THE LIVING and THE DEAD

BY JASON

FANTAGRAPHICS BOOKS • 7563 Lake City Way NE • Seattle WA 98115

DESIGNED by Jason and Covey | PRODUCTION by Jacob Covey
EDITED & TRANSLATED by Kim Thompson | PUBLISHED by Gary Groth and Kim Thompson

Special thanks to Erik Falk at Jippi Comics.

To receive a free catalog of comics, call 1-800-657-1100 or write us at the above address.

Distributed in the U.S. by W.W. Norton and Company, Inc. (212-354-5500) • Distributed in Canada by Raincoast Books (800-663-5714) • Distributed in the United Kingdom by Turnaround Distribution (208-829-3009)

Visit the website for Jippi, who originally publishes Jason's work, at www.jippicomics.com
Visit the website for The Beguiling, where Jason's original artwork can be purchased: www.beguiling.com
Visit the Fantagraphics website, just because: www.fantagraphics.com

---

FIRST PRINTING: December 2006 • ISBN: 978-1-56097-794-0 • PRINTED in China

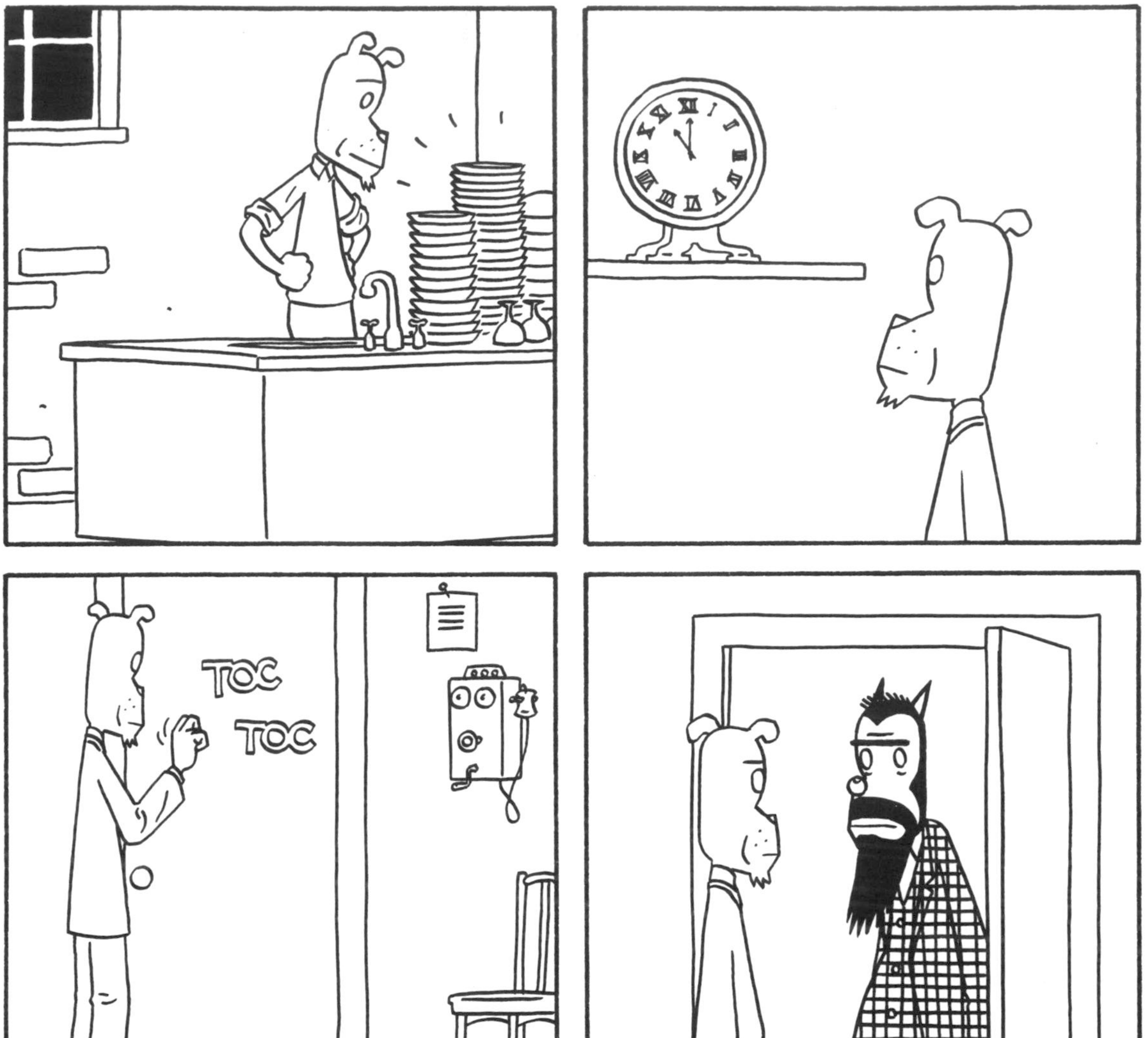
TOC
TOC
Don't spend it all
in one place!

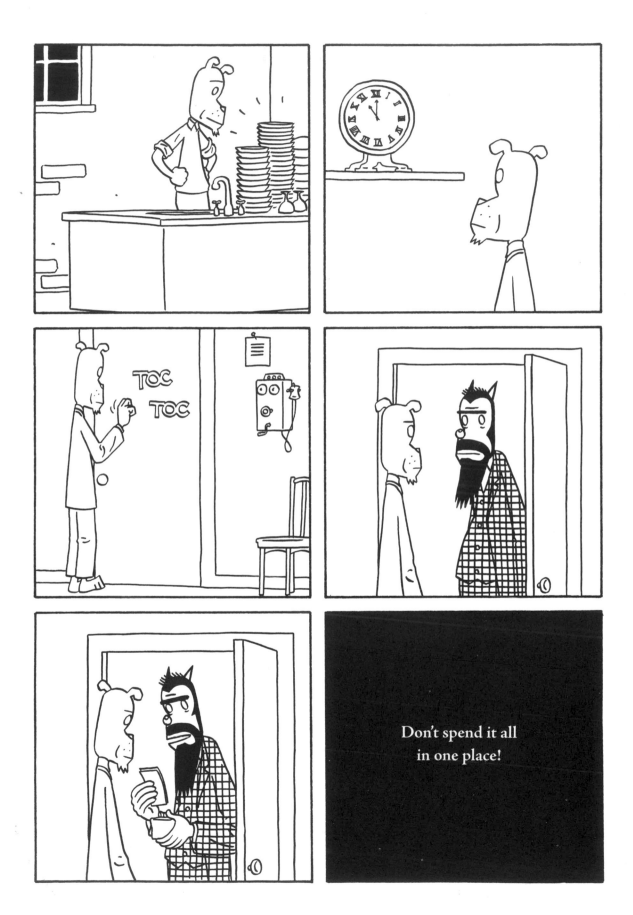

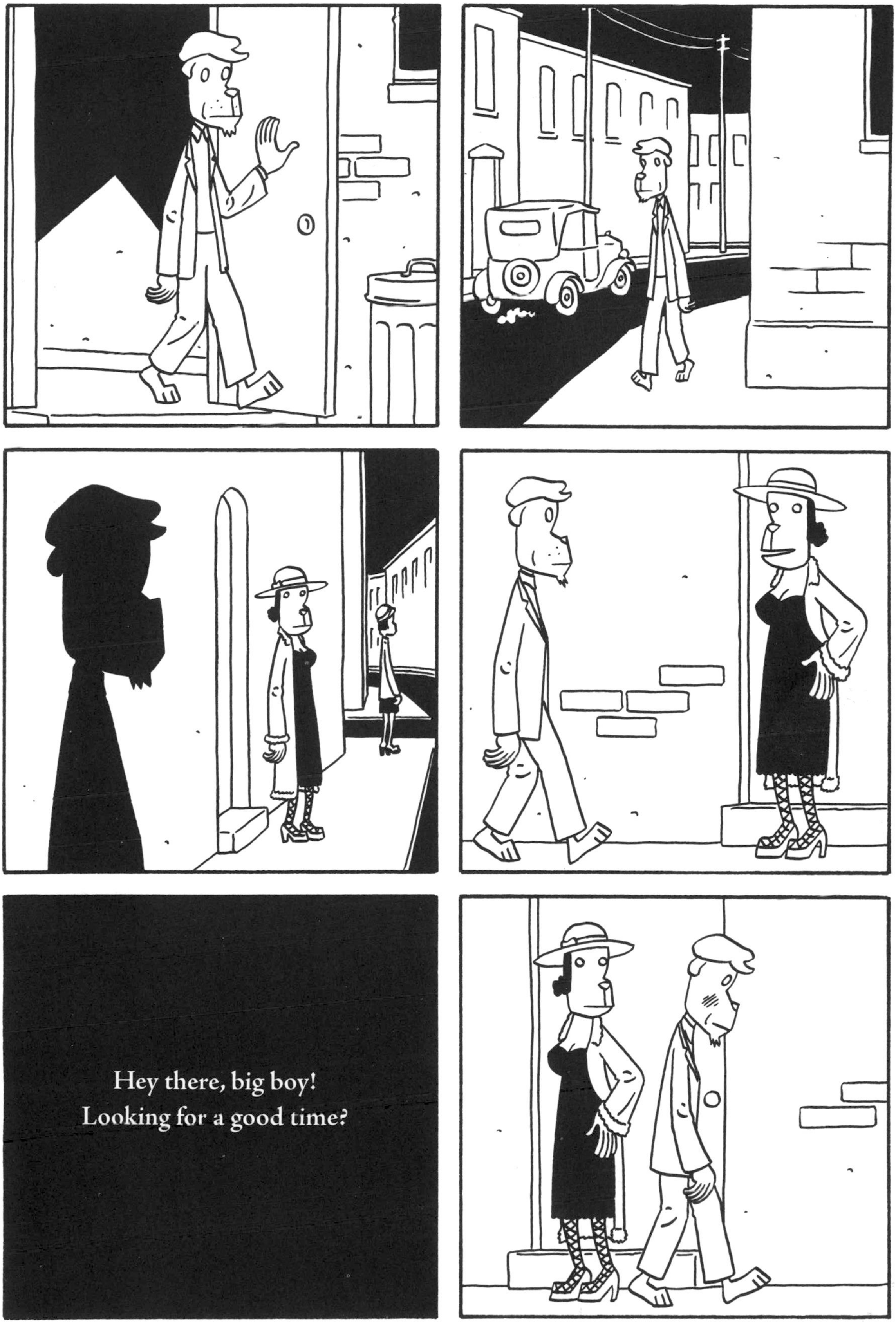
Hey there, big boy!
Looking for a good time?

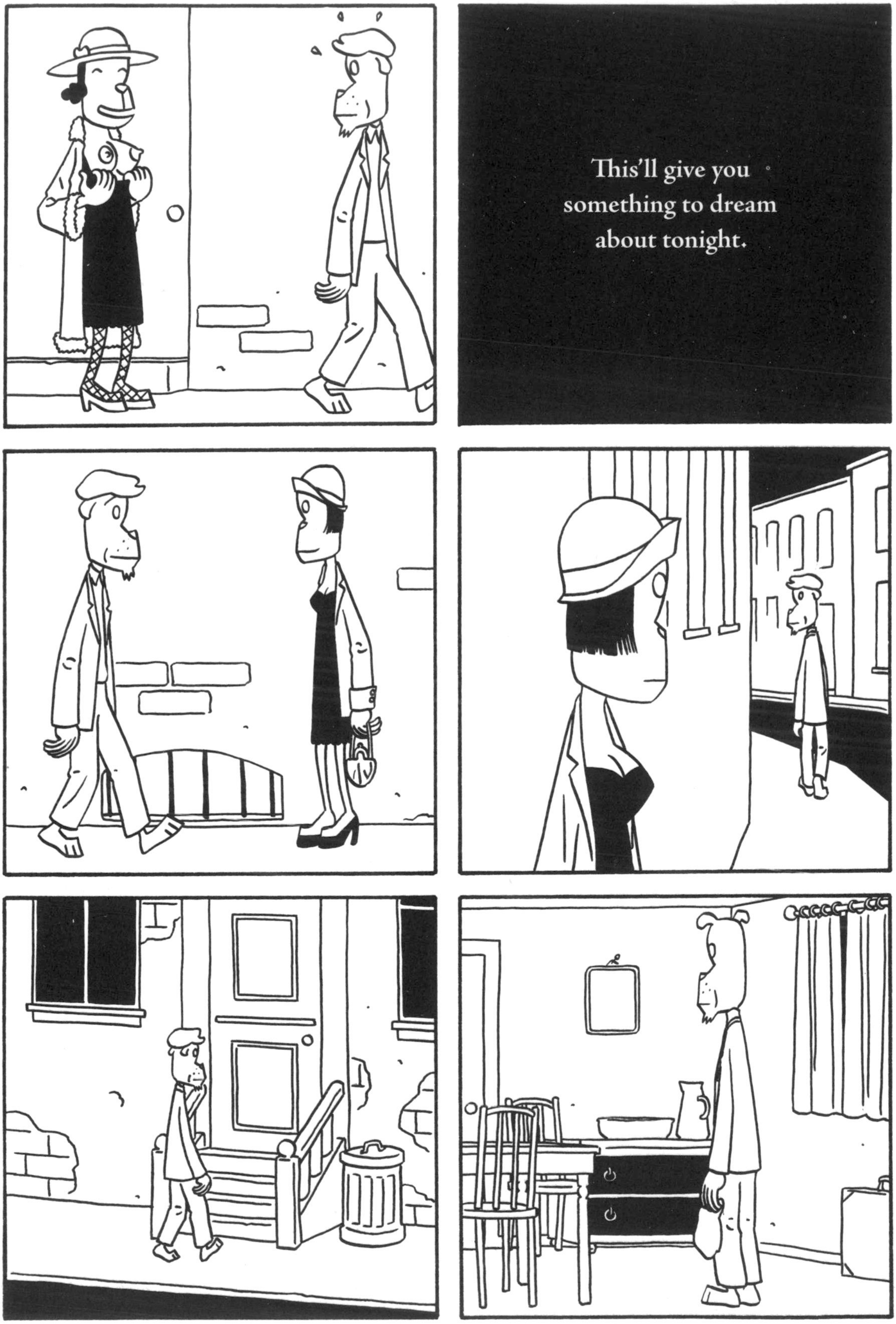
This'll give you something to dream about tonight.

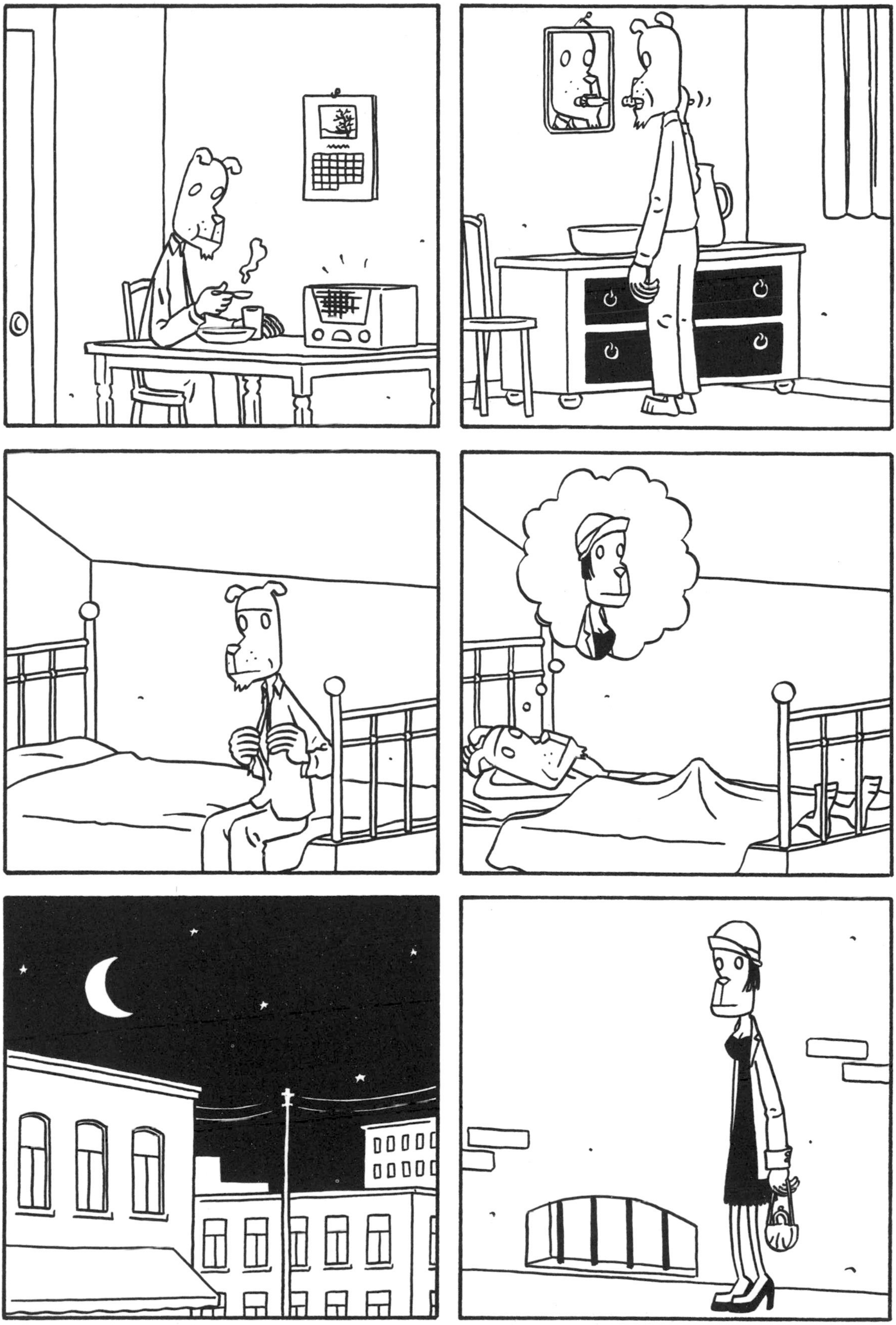

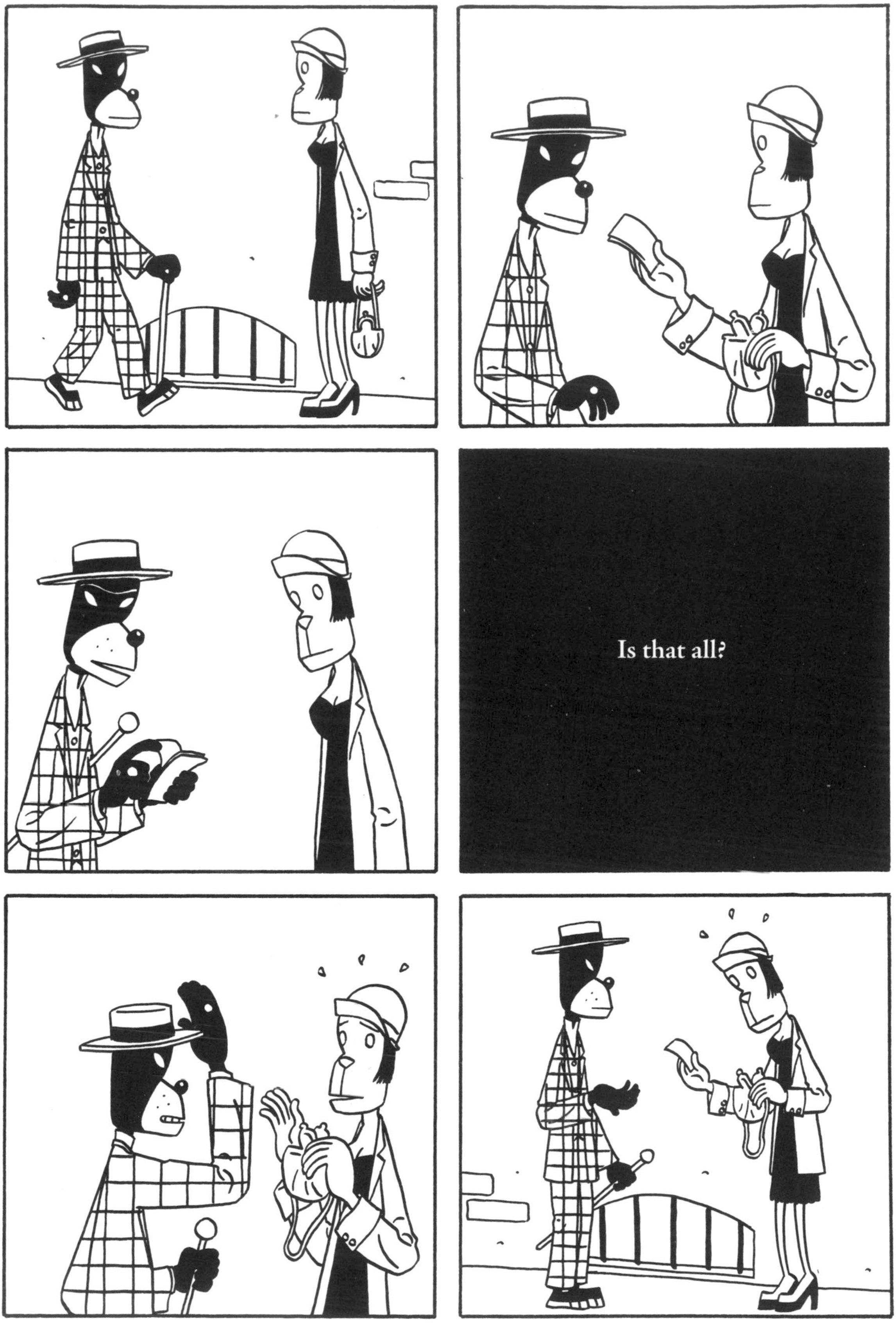
Is that all?

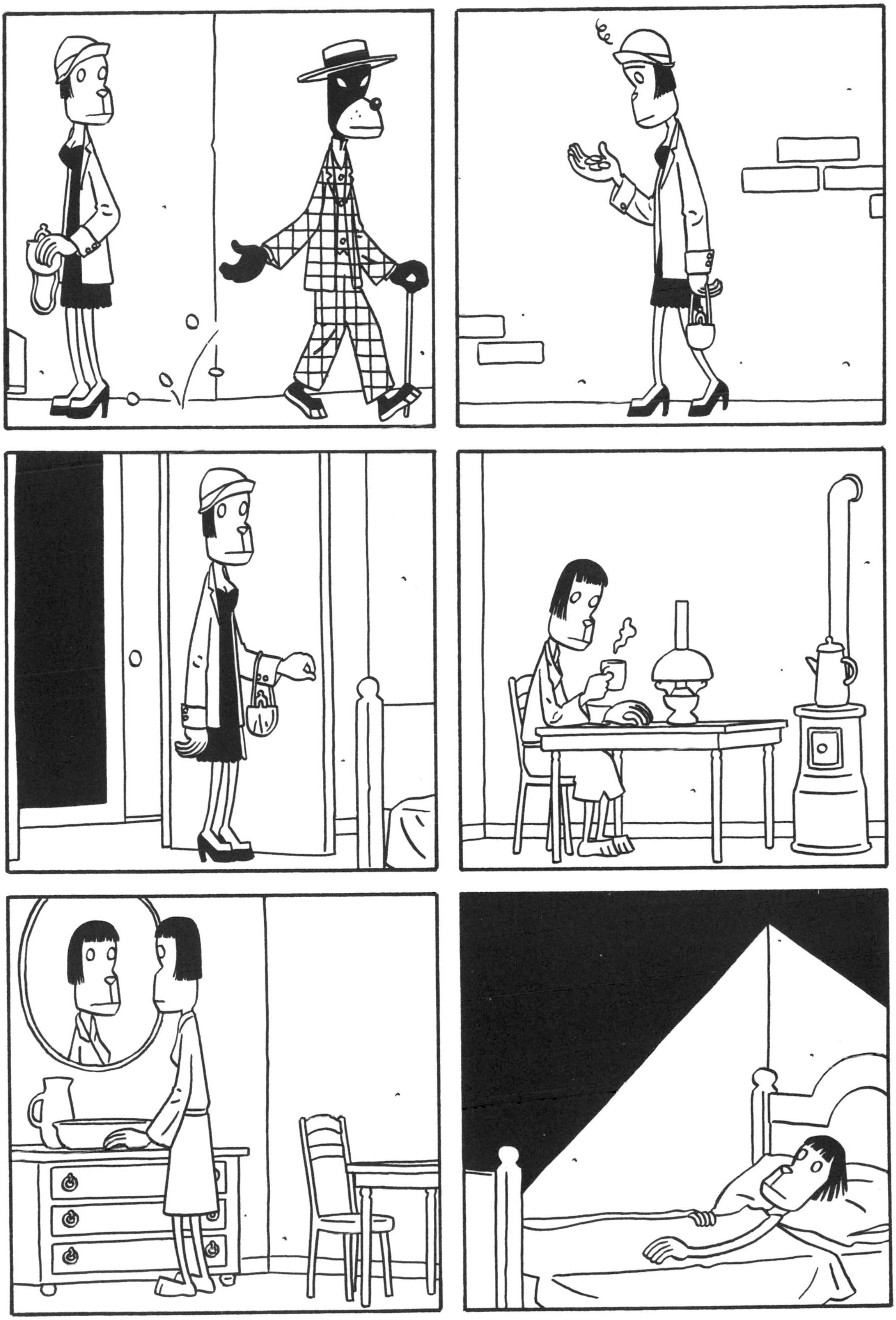

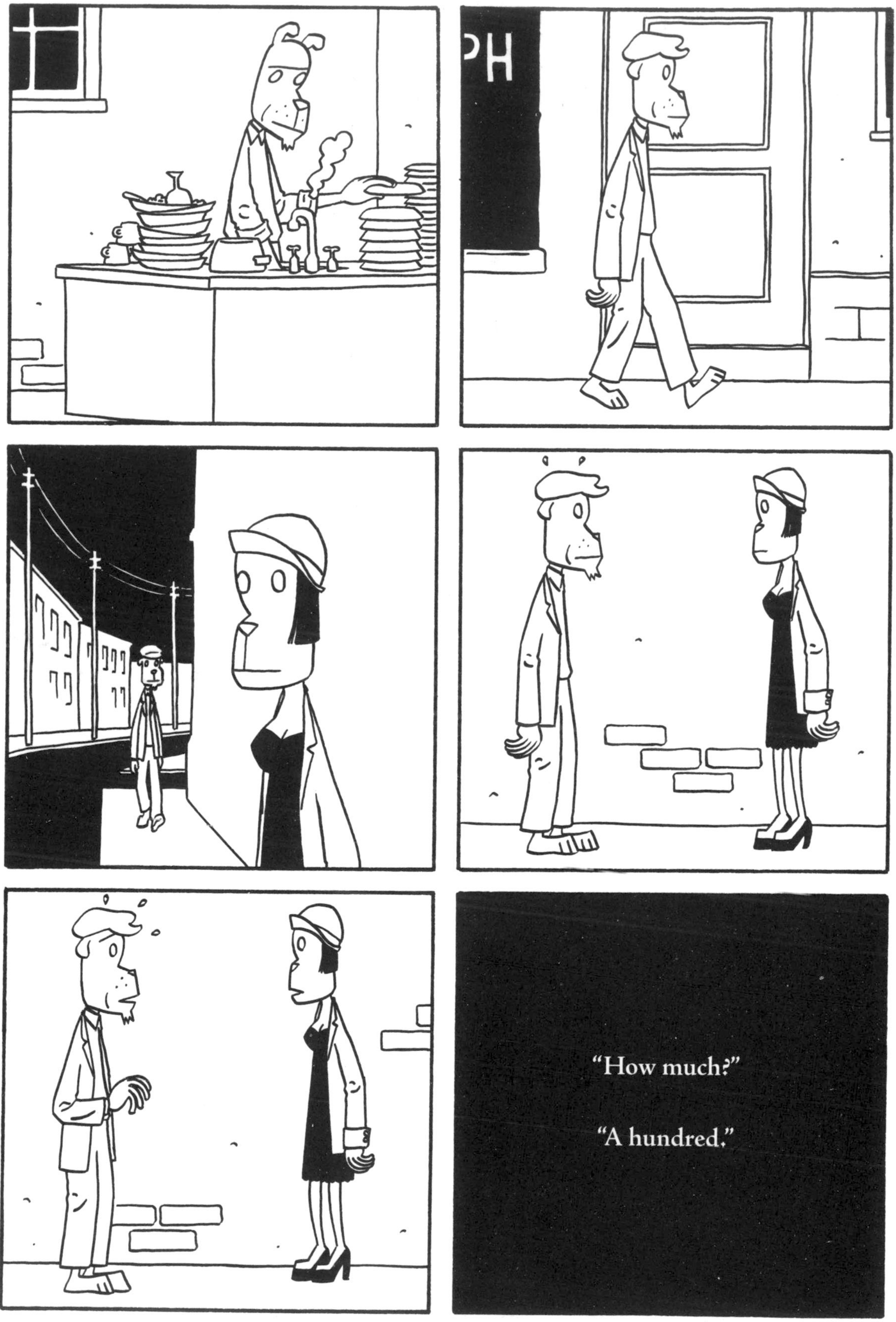
PH
"How much?"
"A hundred."

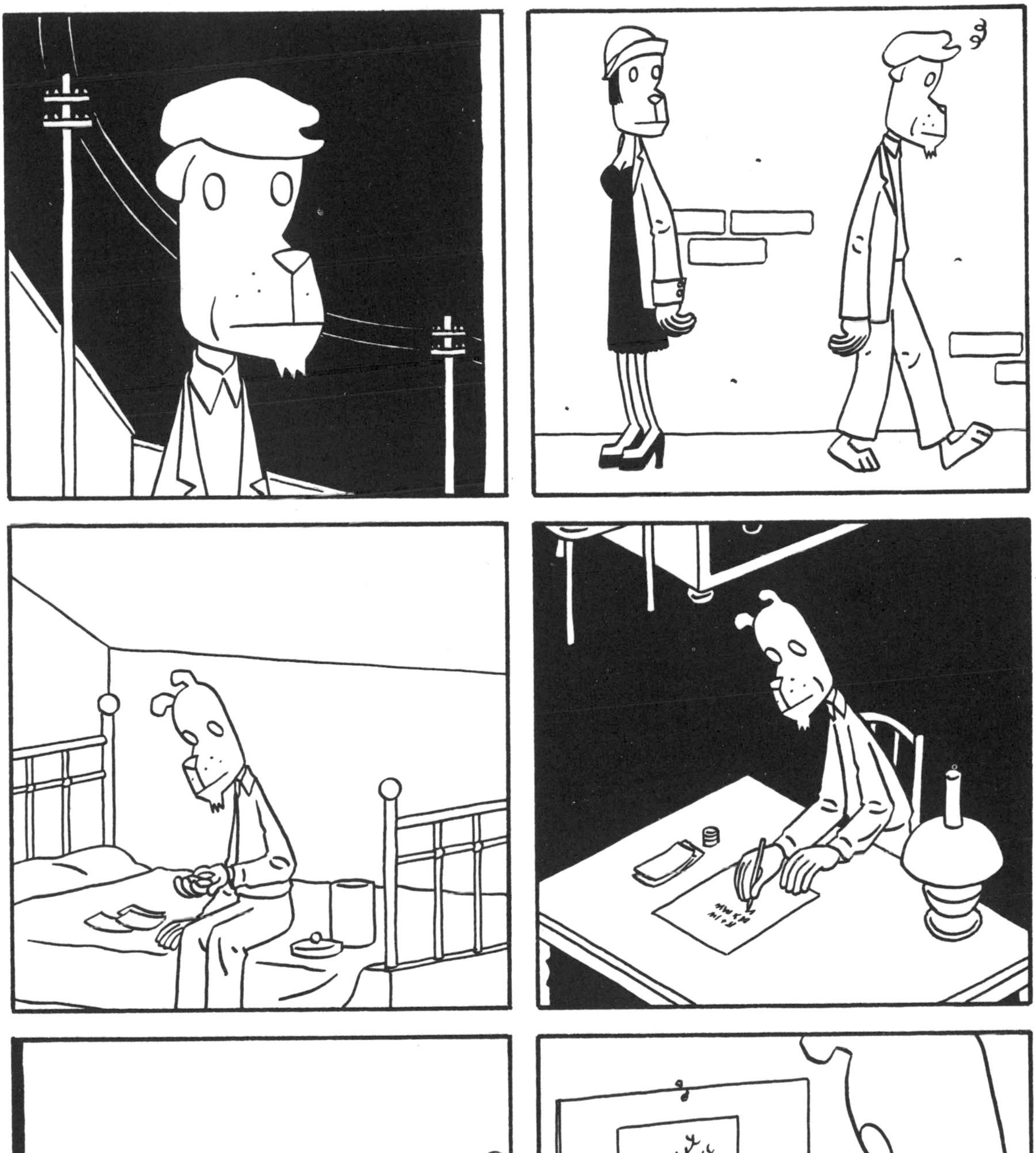

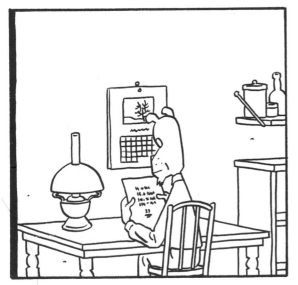

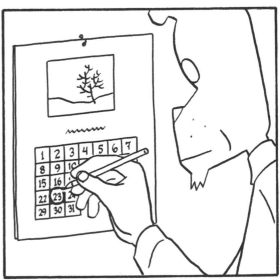

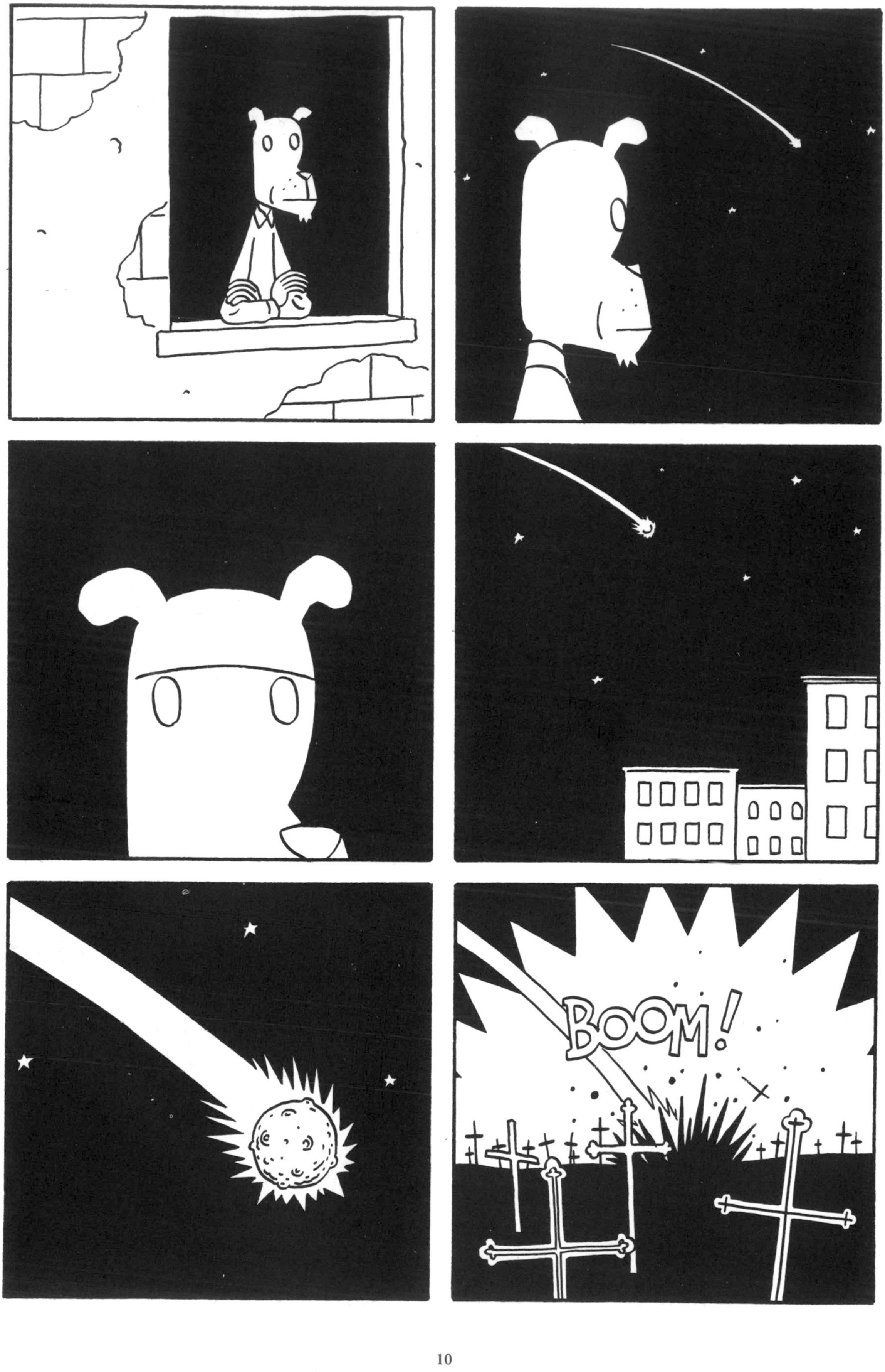
BOOM!

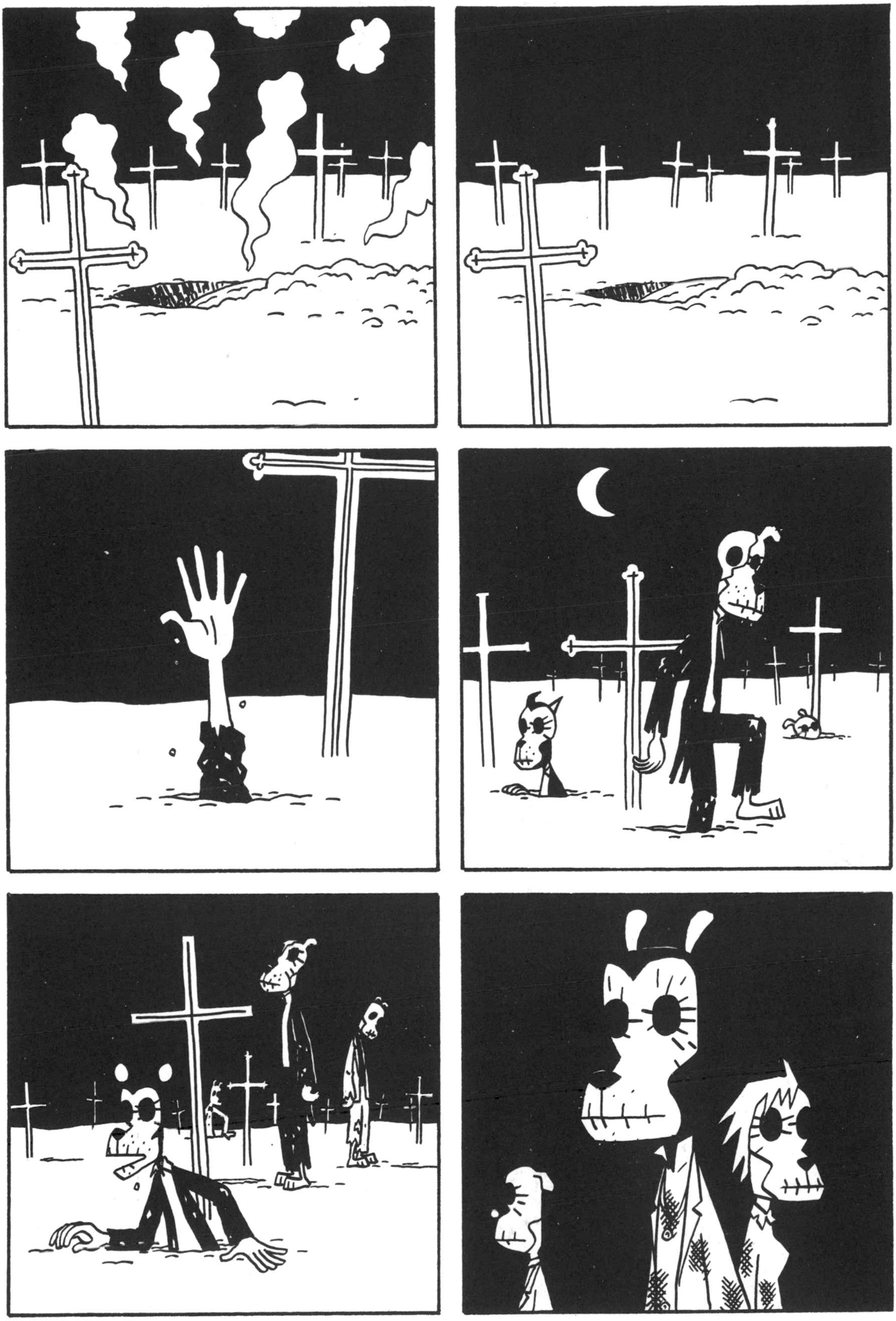

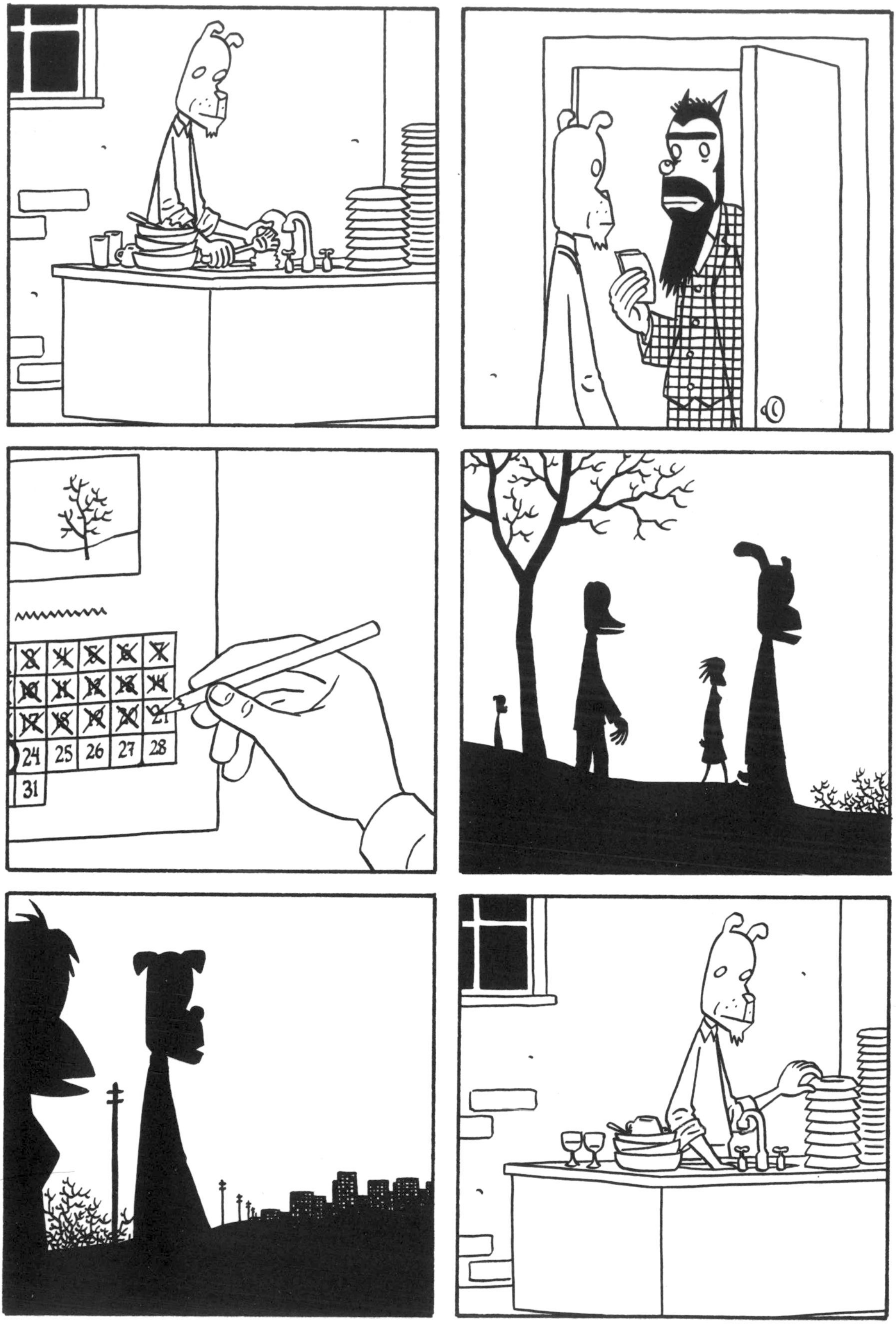
21
24 25 26 27 28
31

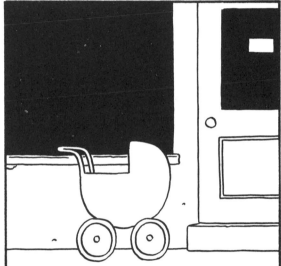

CIGARS

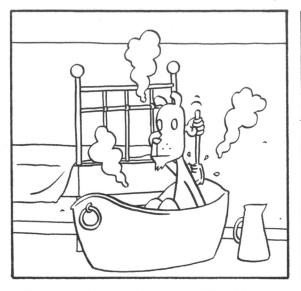

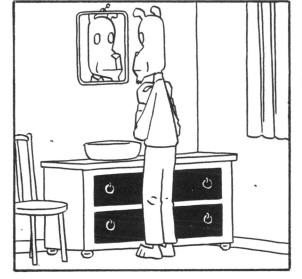

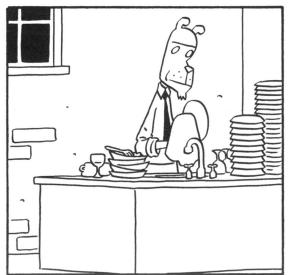

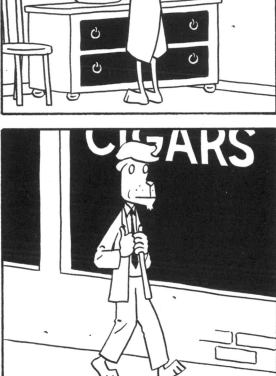

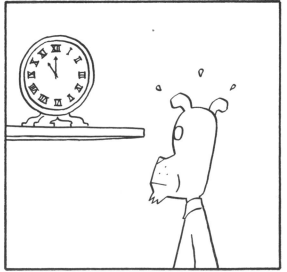

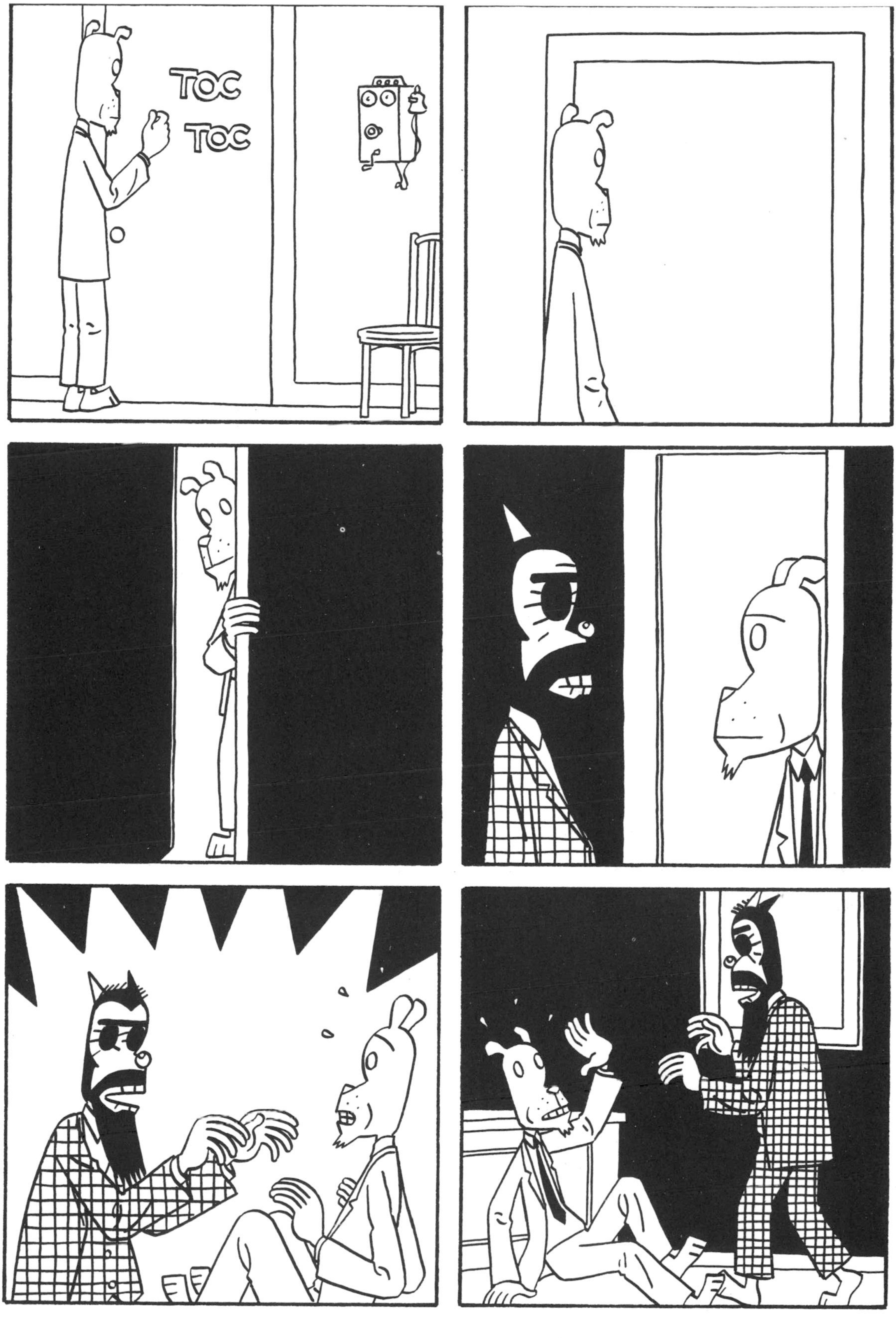
TOC
TOC

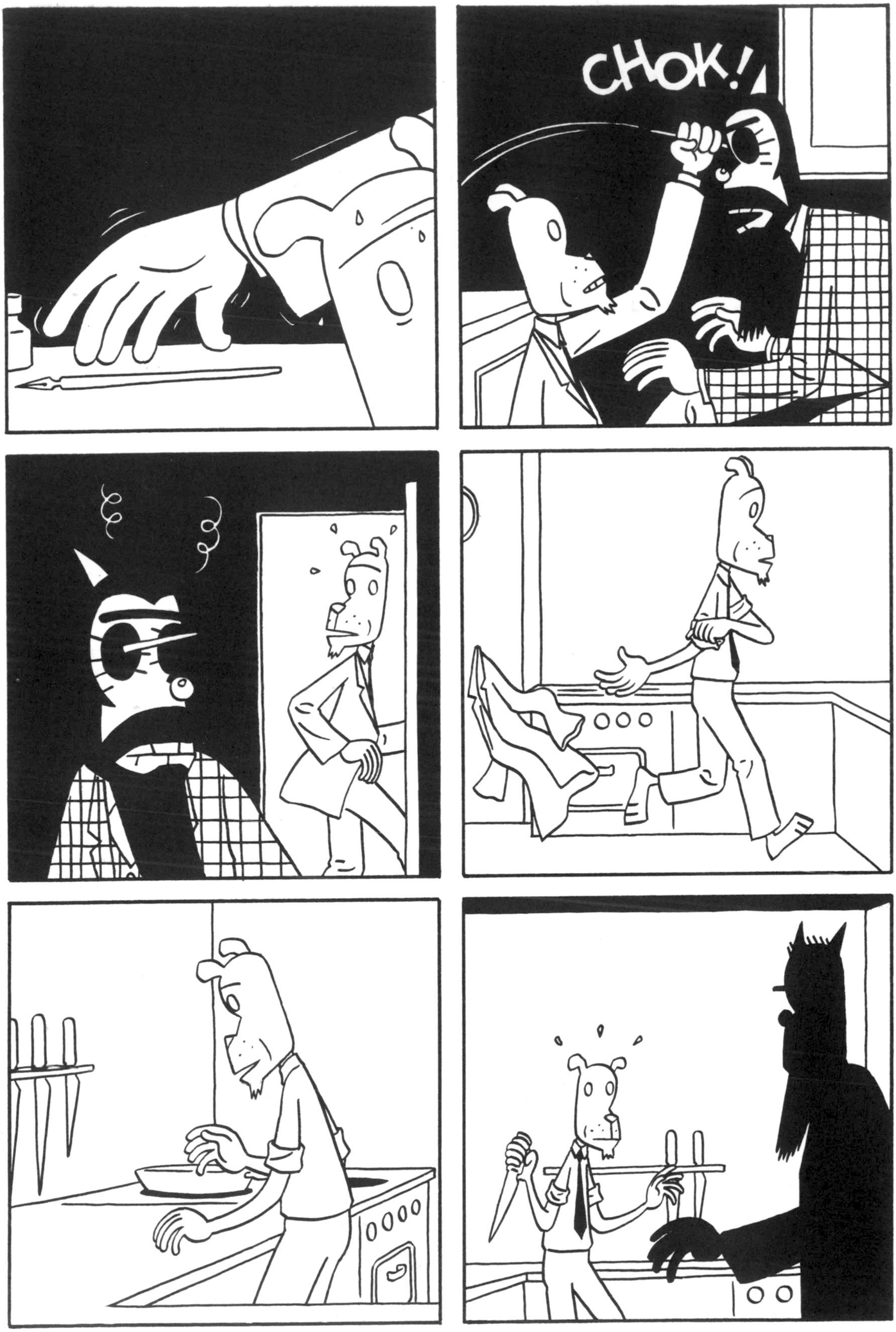
CHOK!

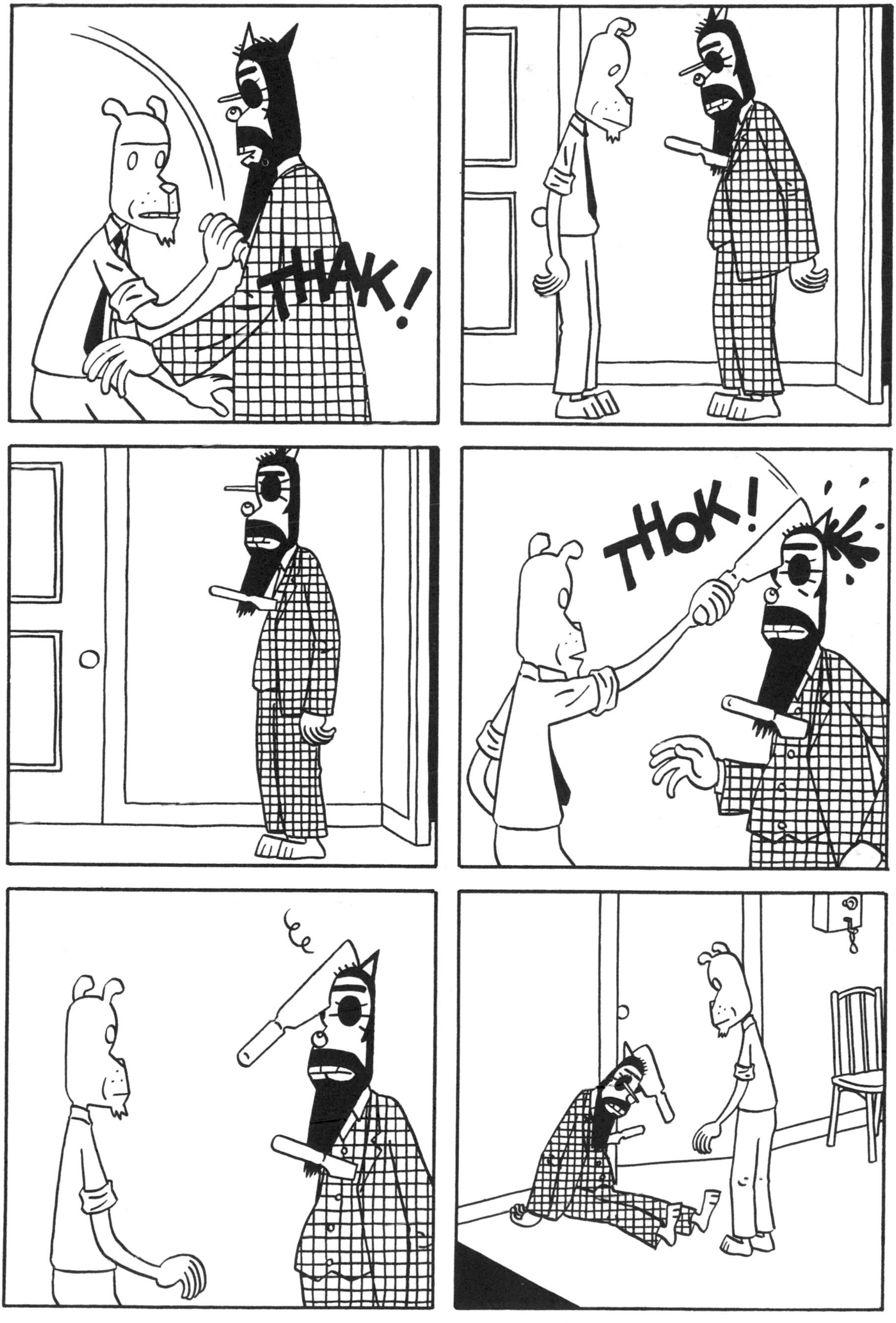
THAK!
THOK!

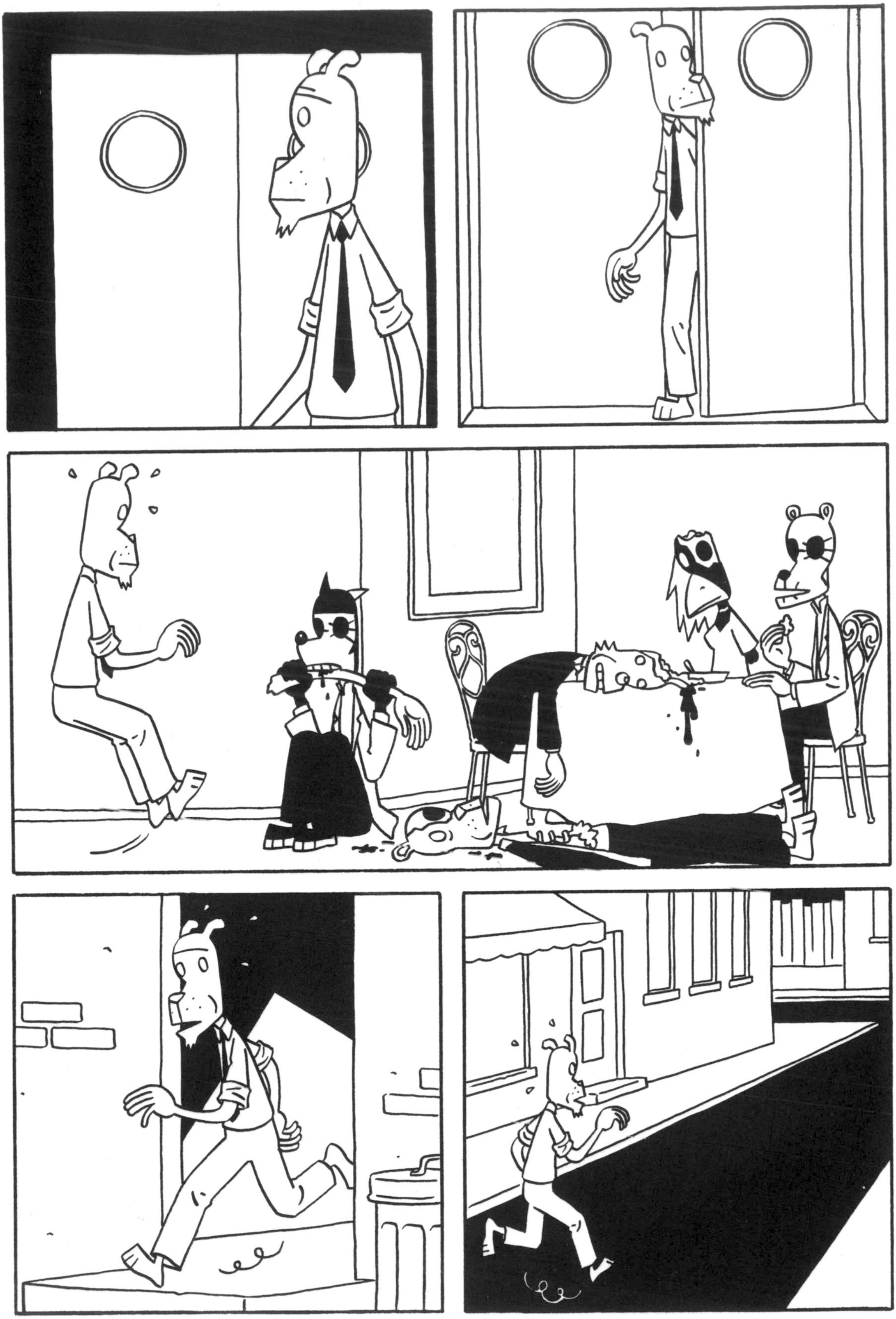

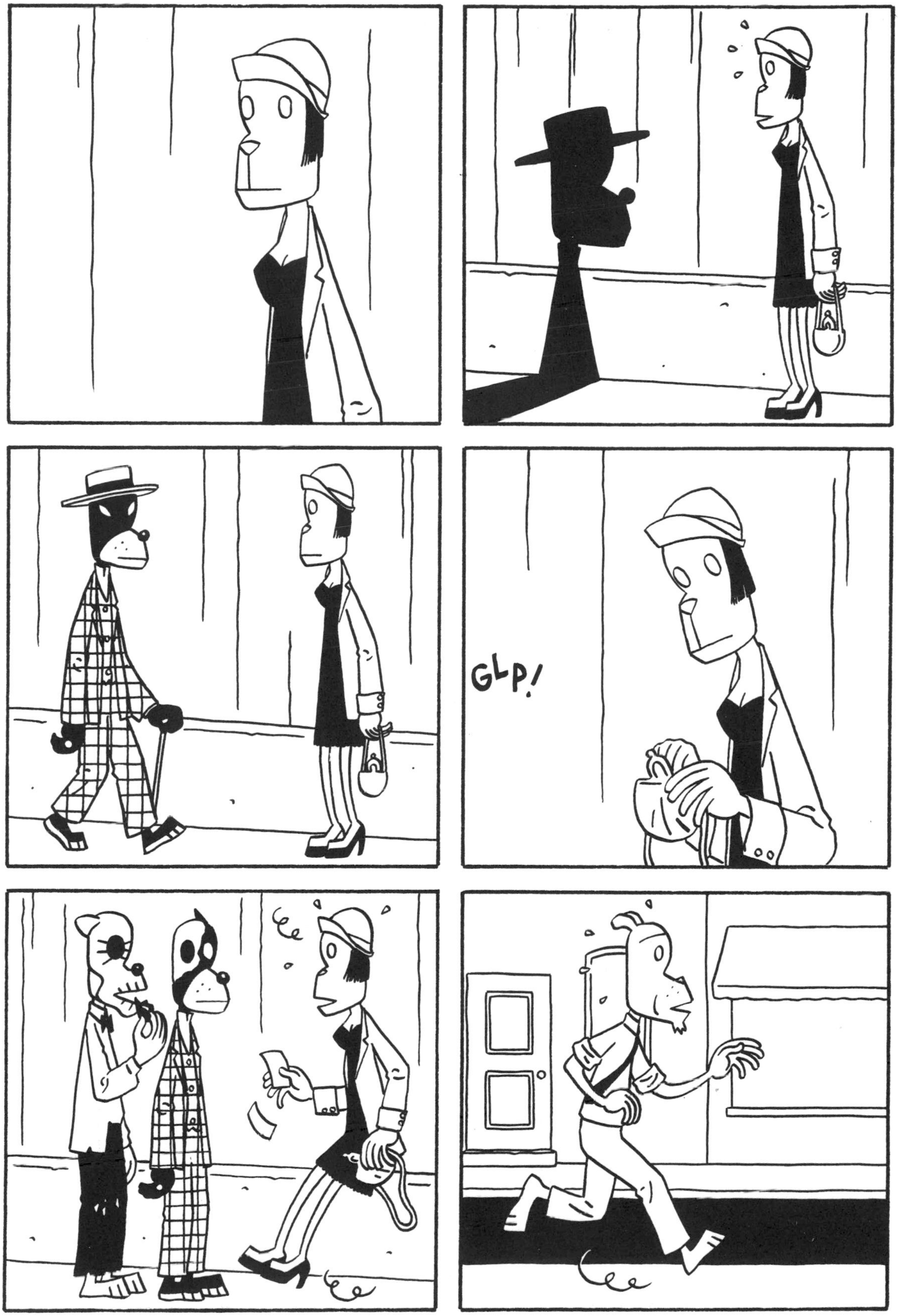
GLP!

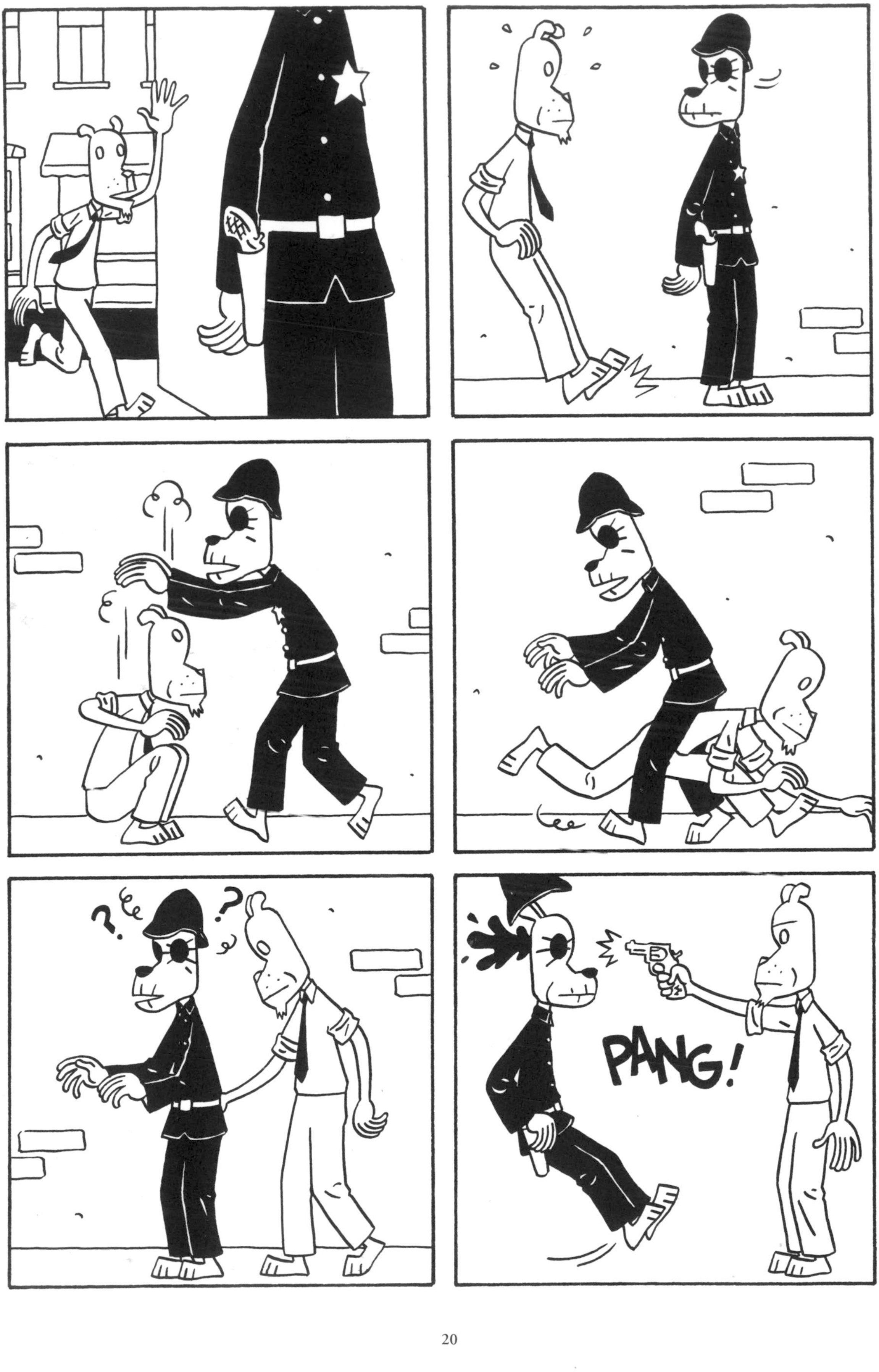
PANG!

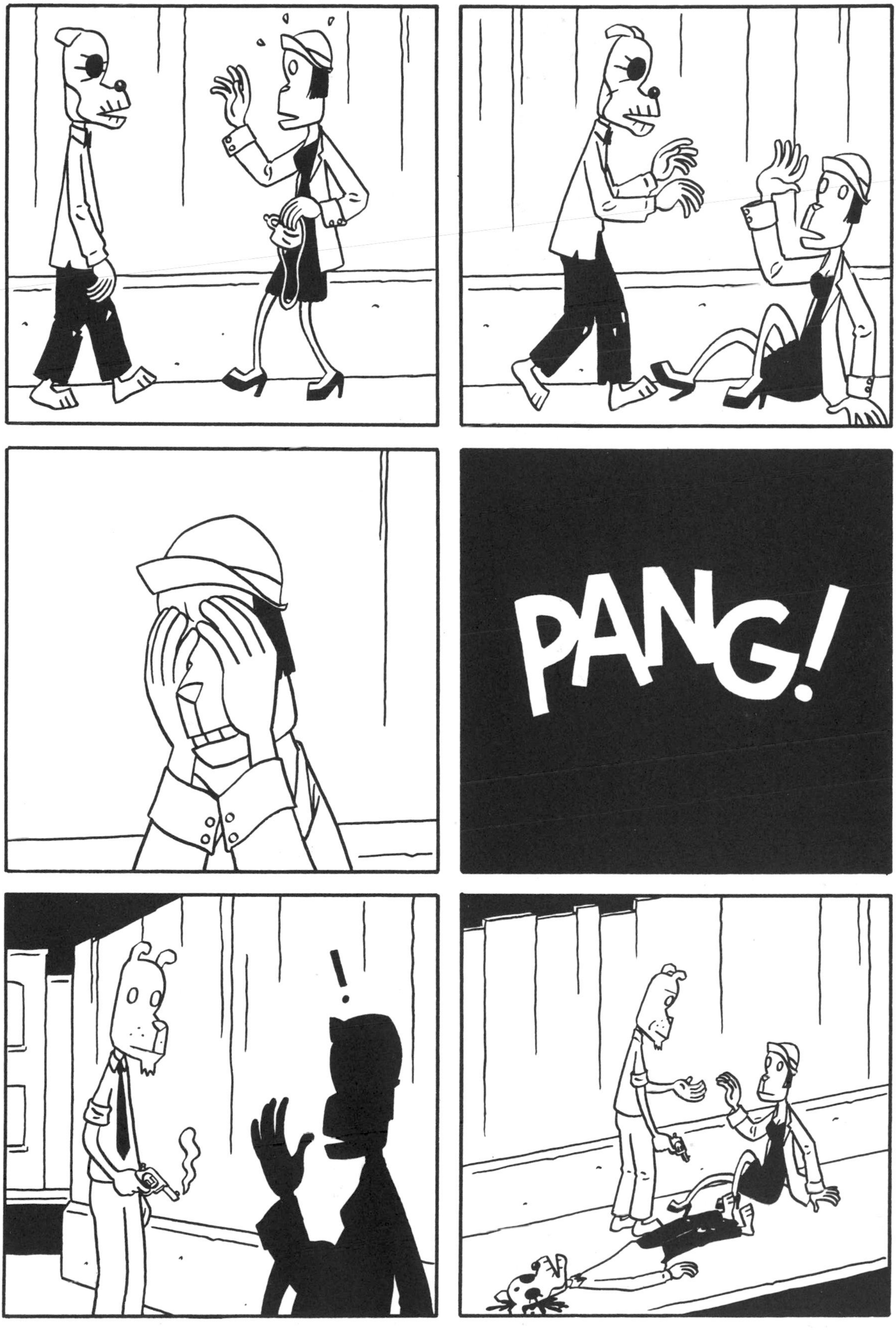
PANG!
!

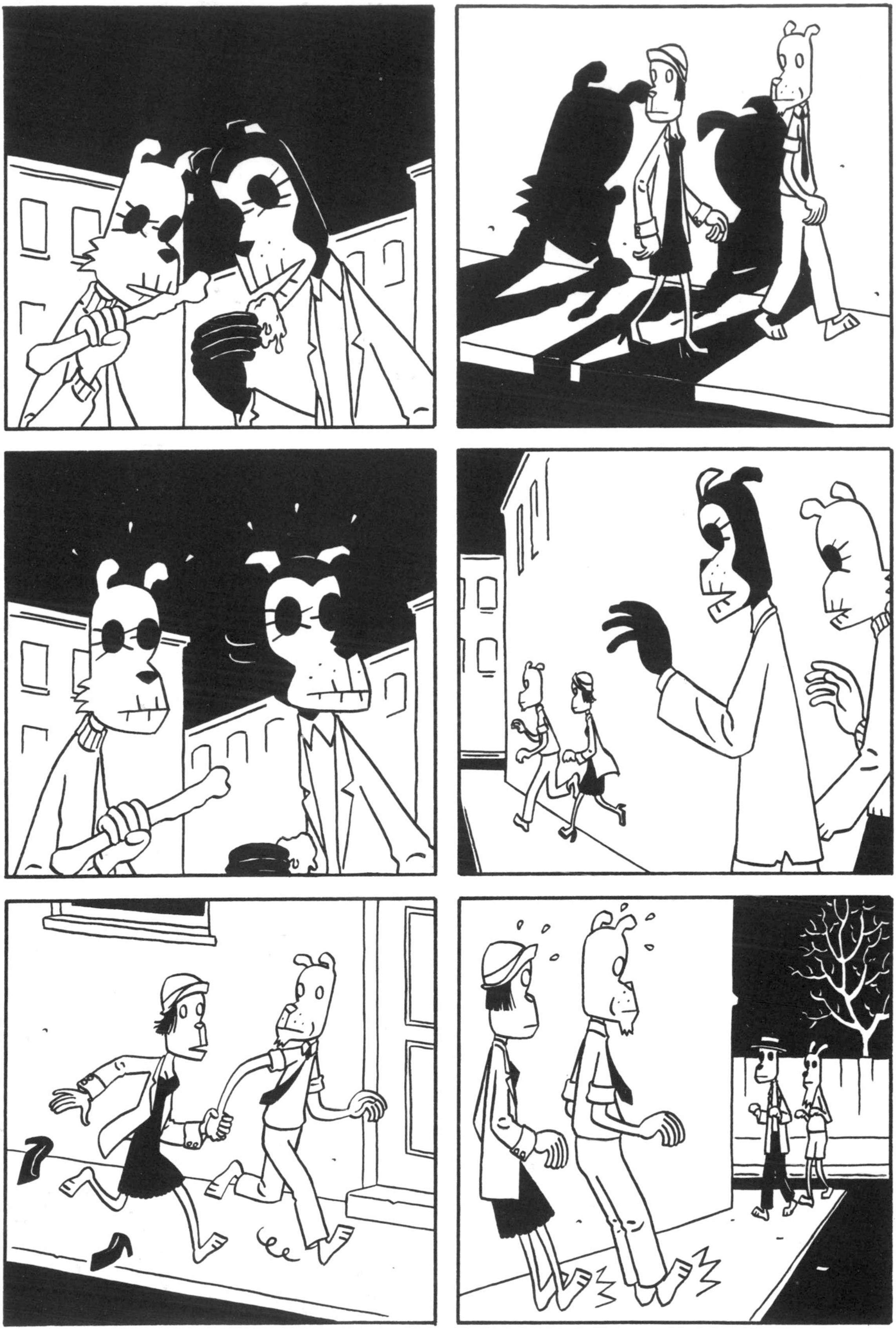

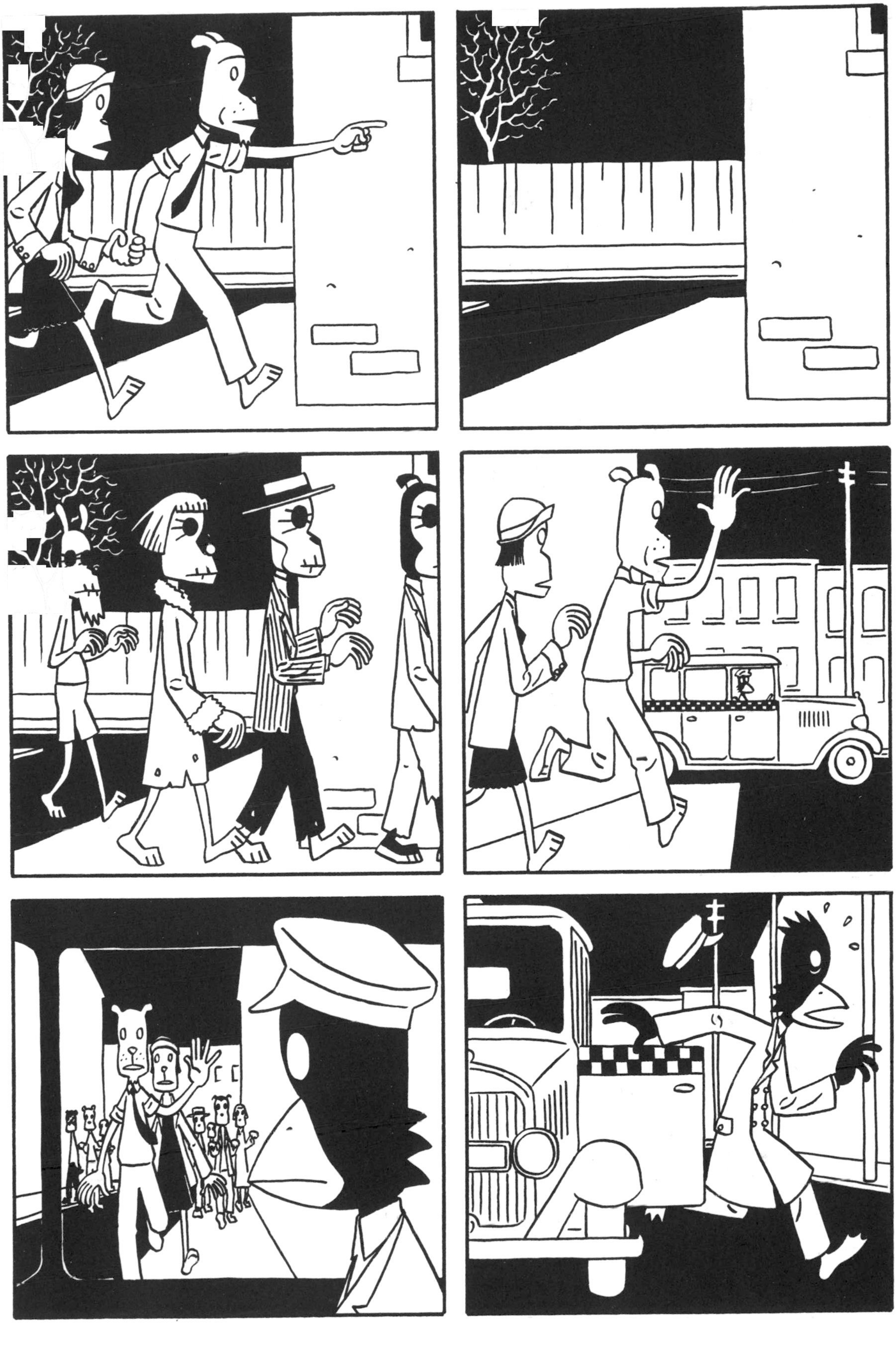

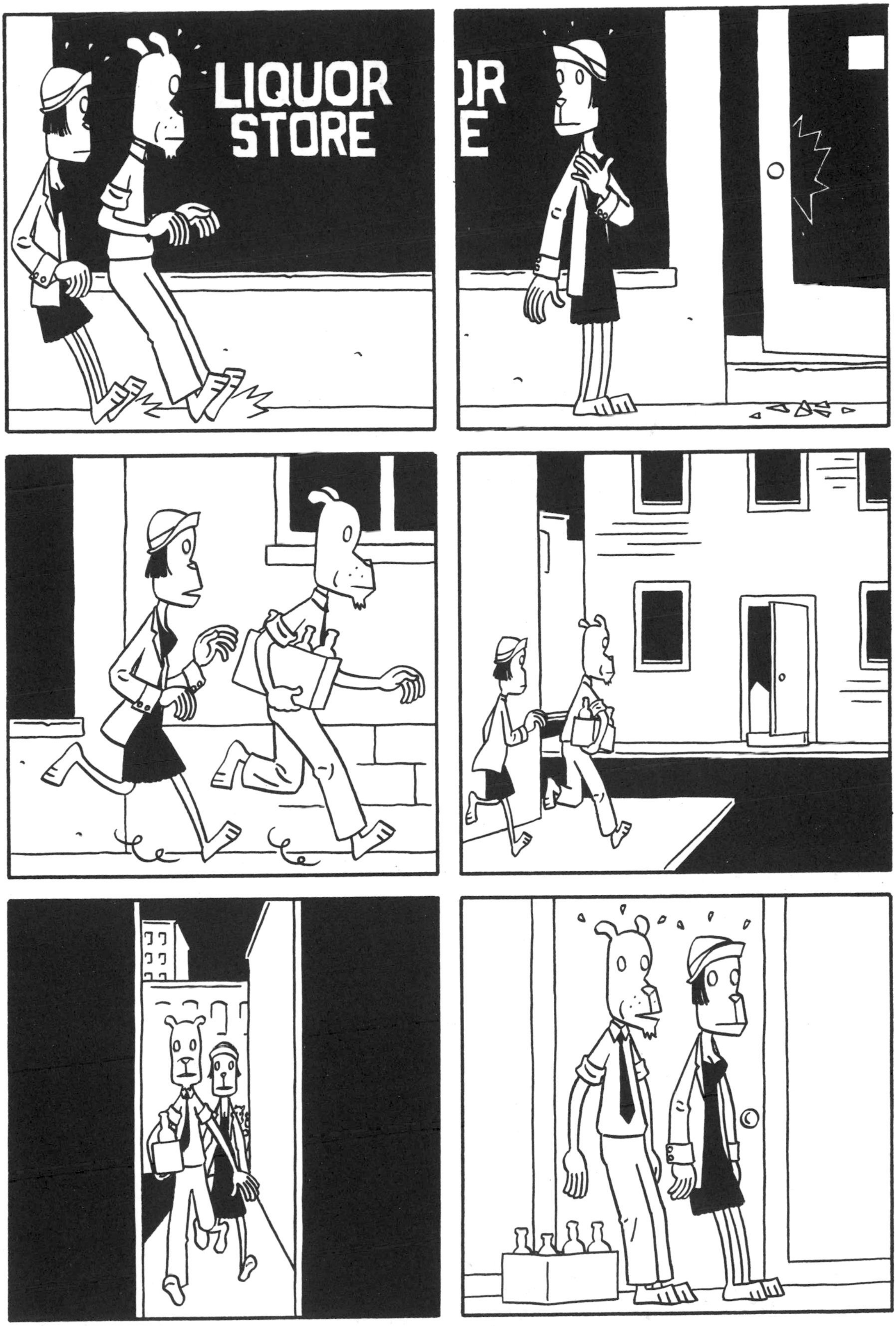
LIQUOR
STORE
OR
E

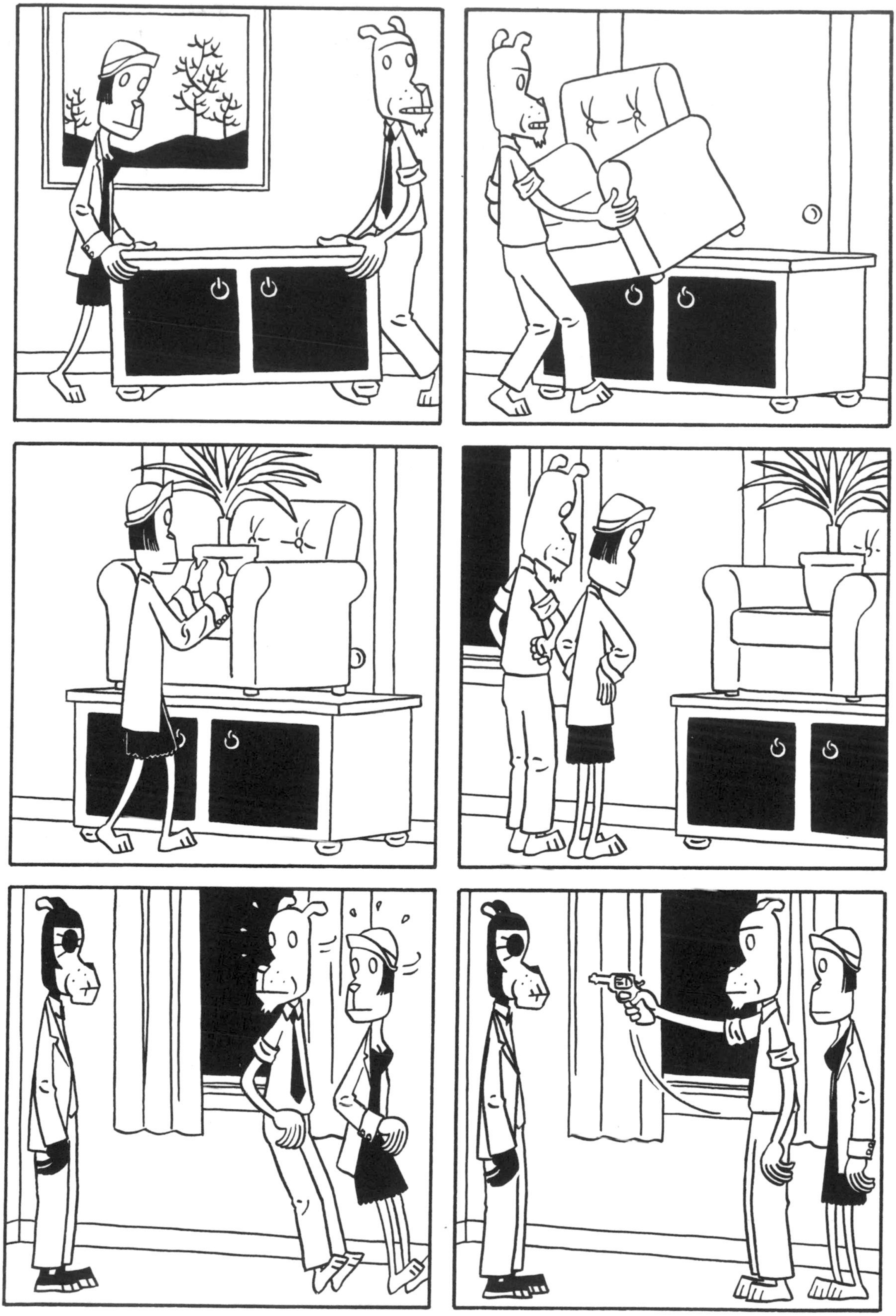

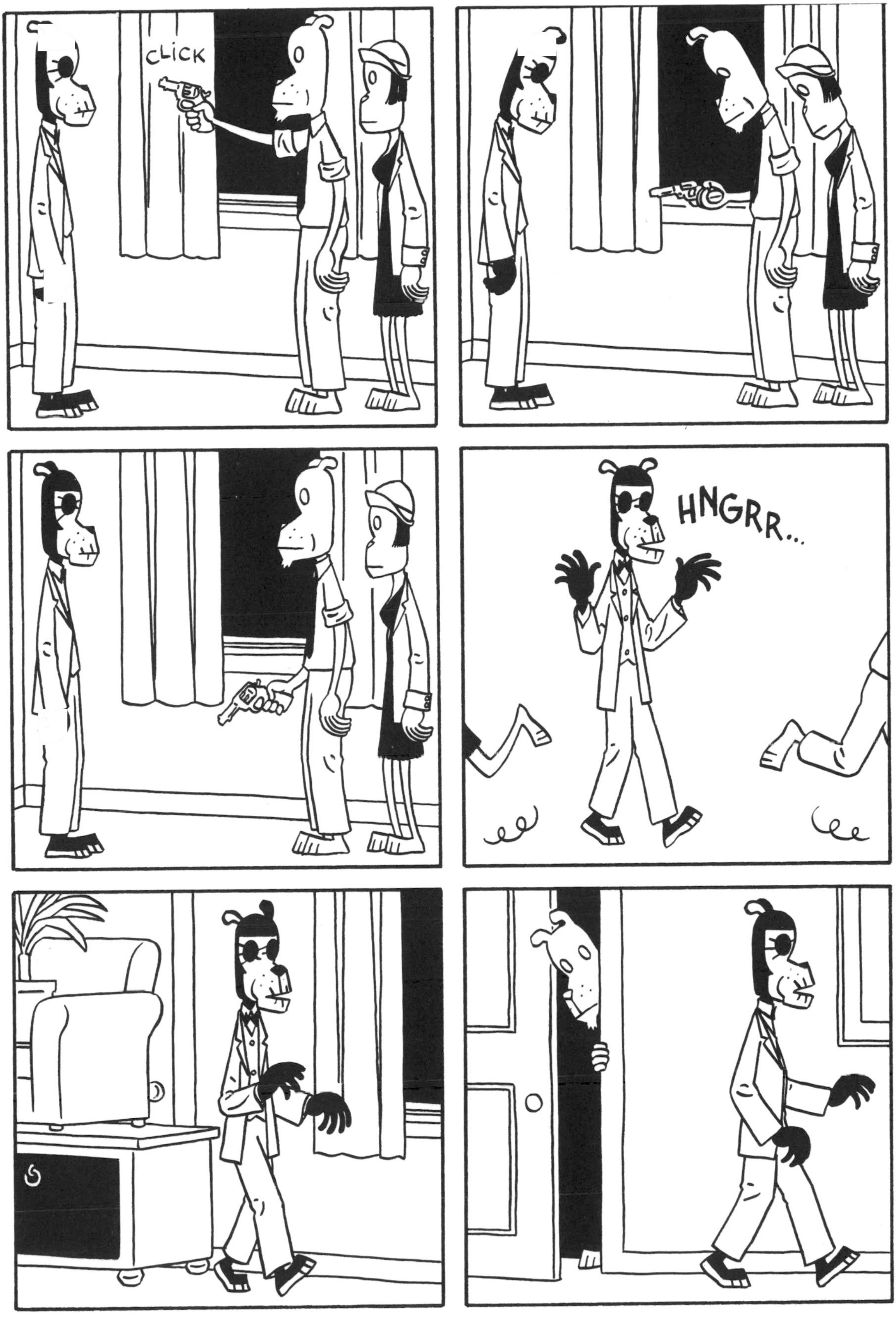
CLICK
HNGRR...

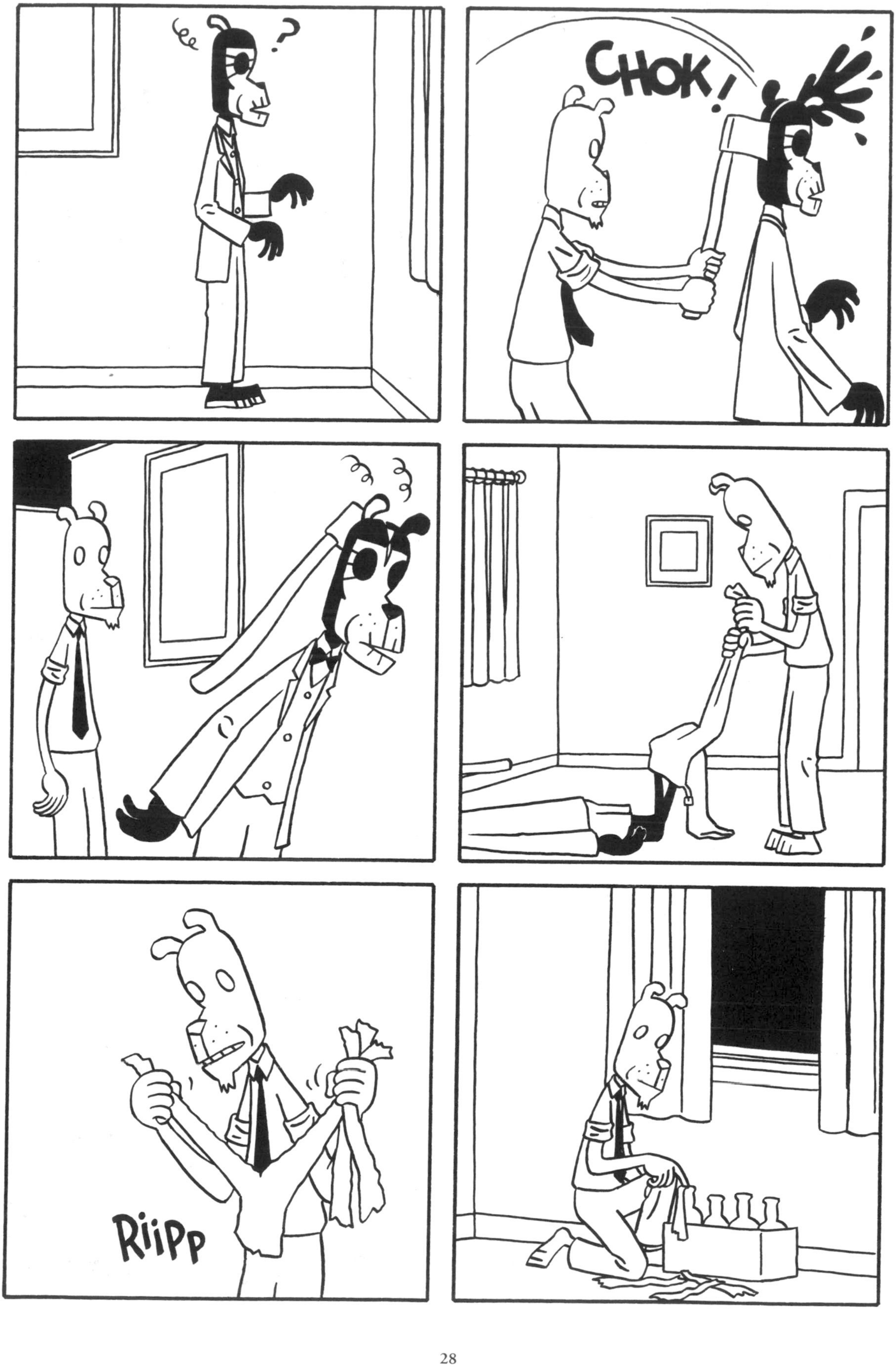
CHOK!
RIIPP

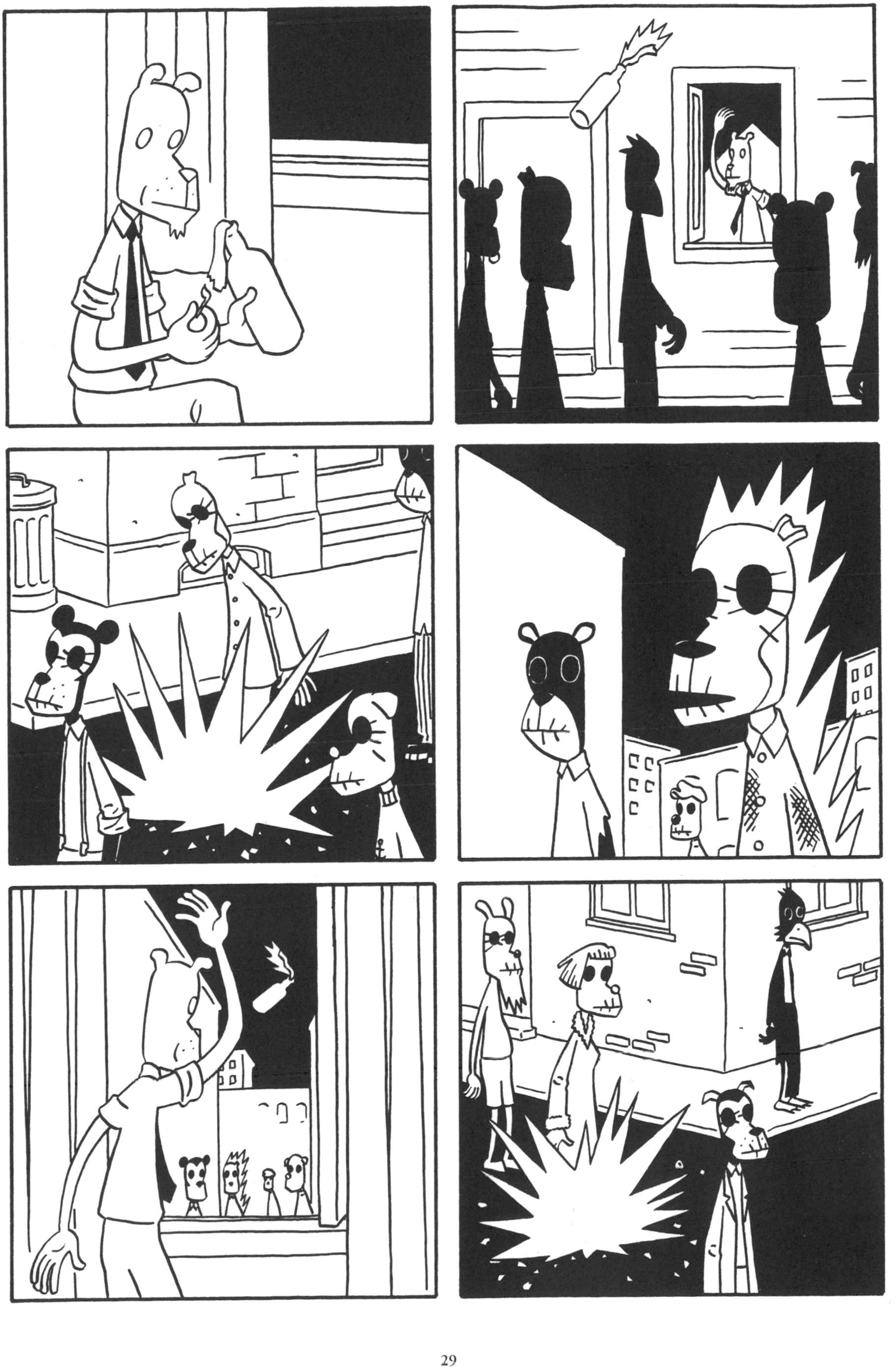

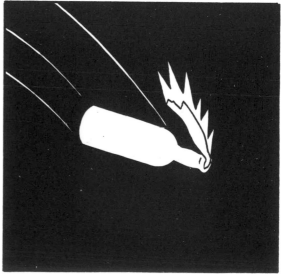

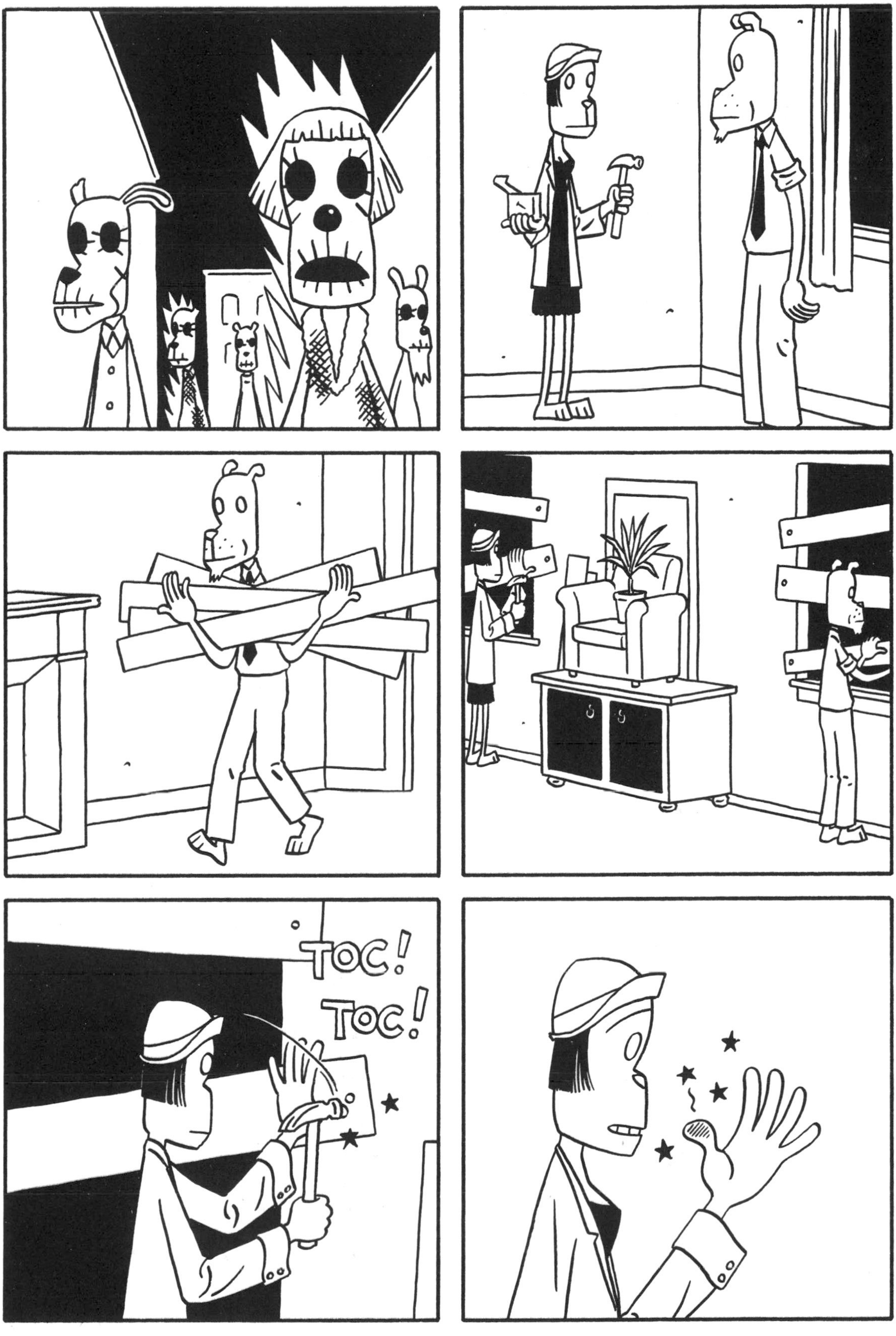
TOC!
TOC!

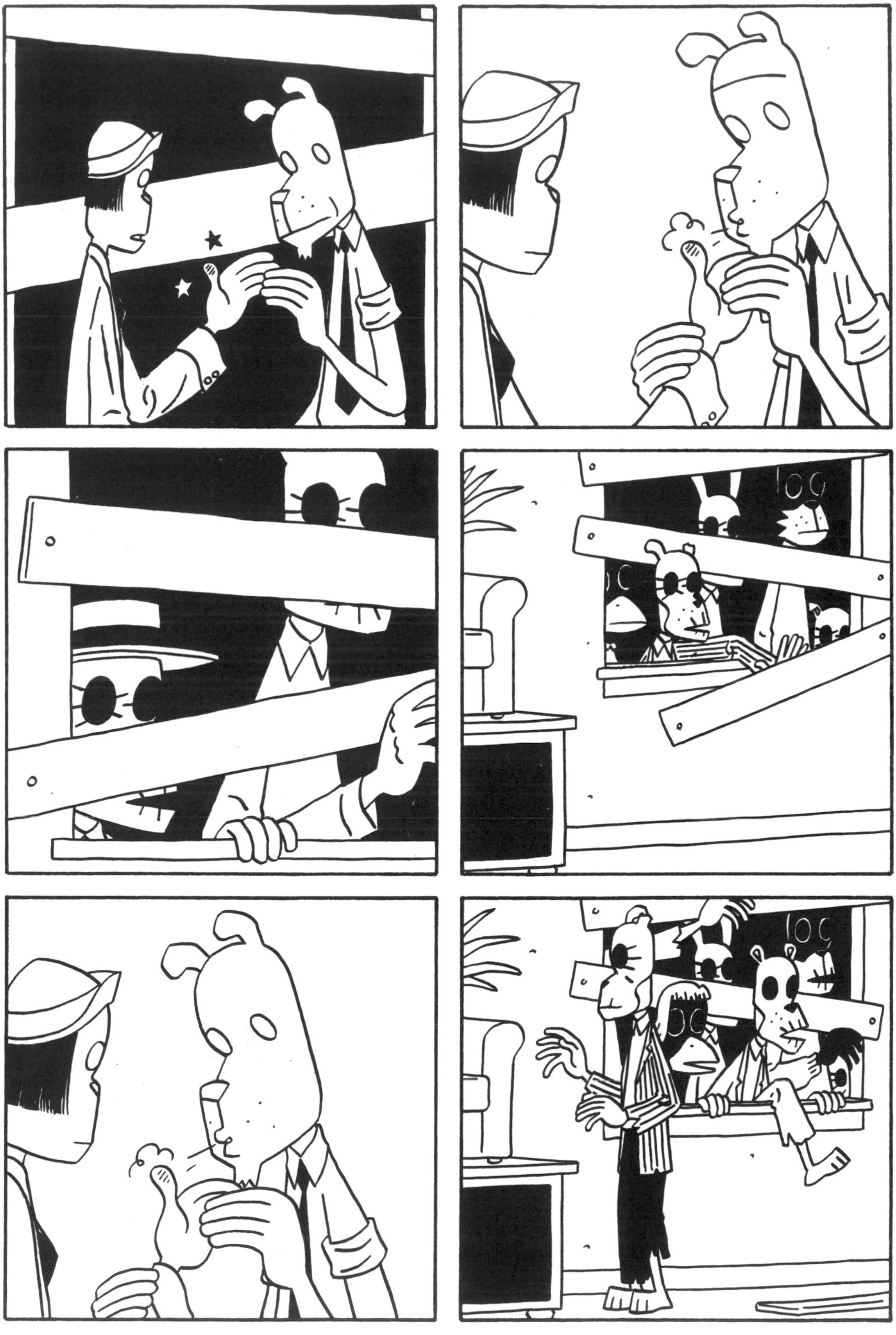

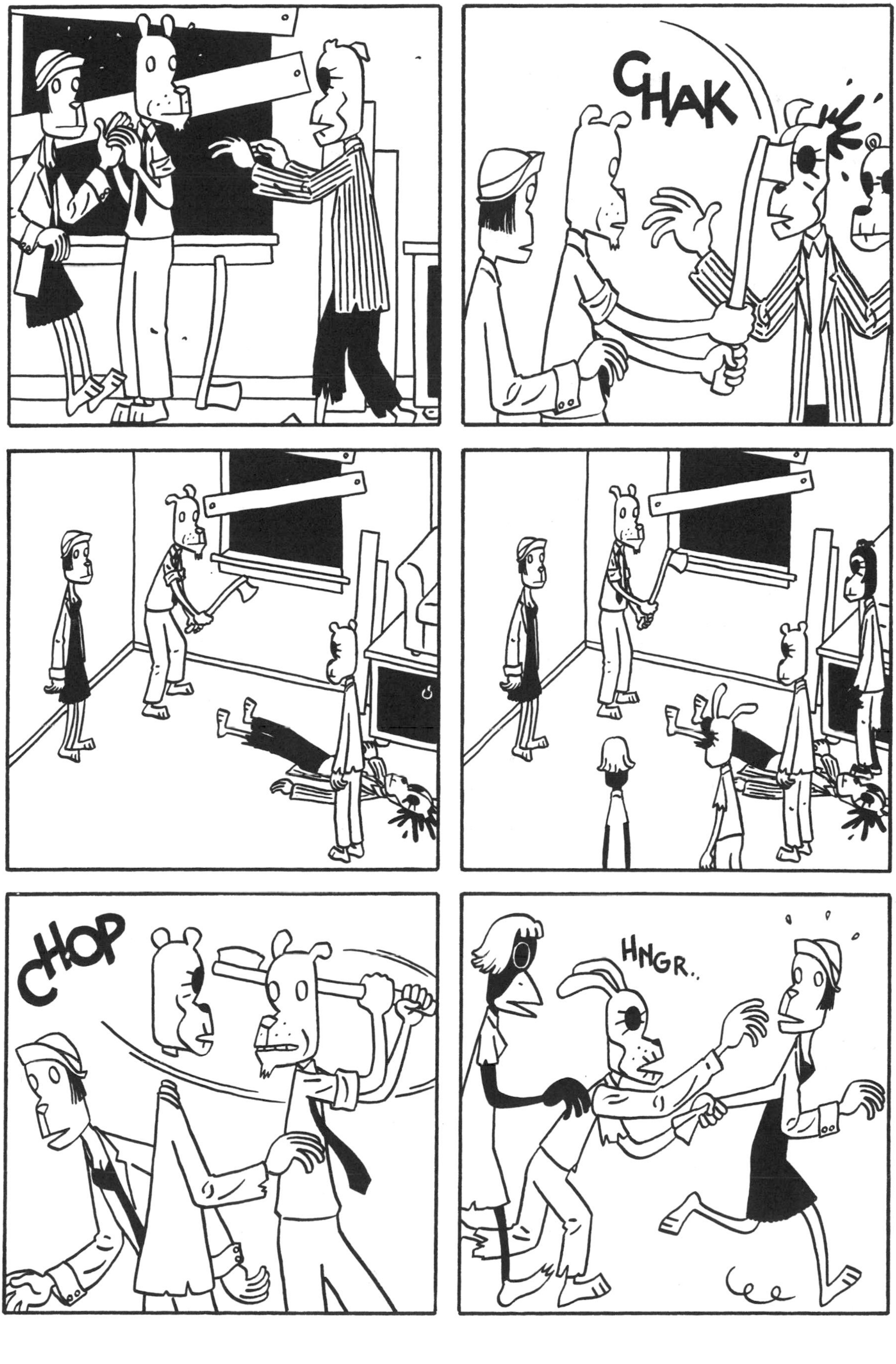
CHAK
CHOP
HNGR..

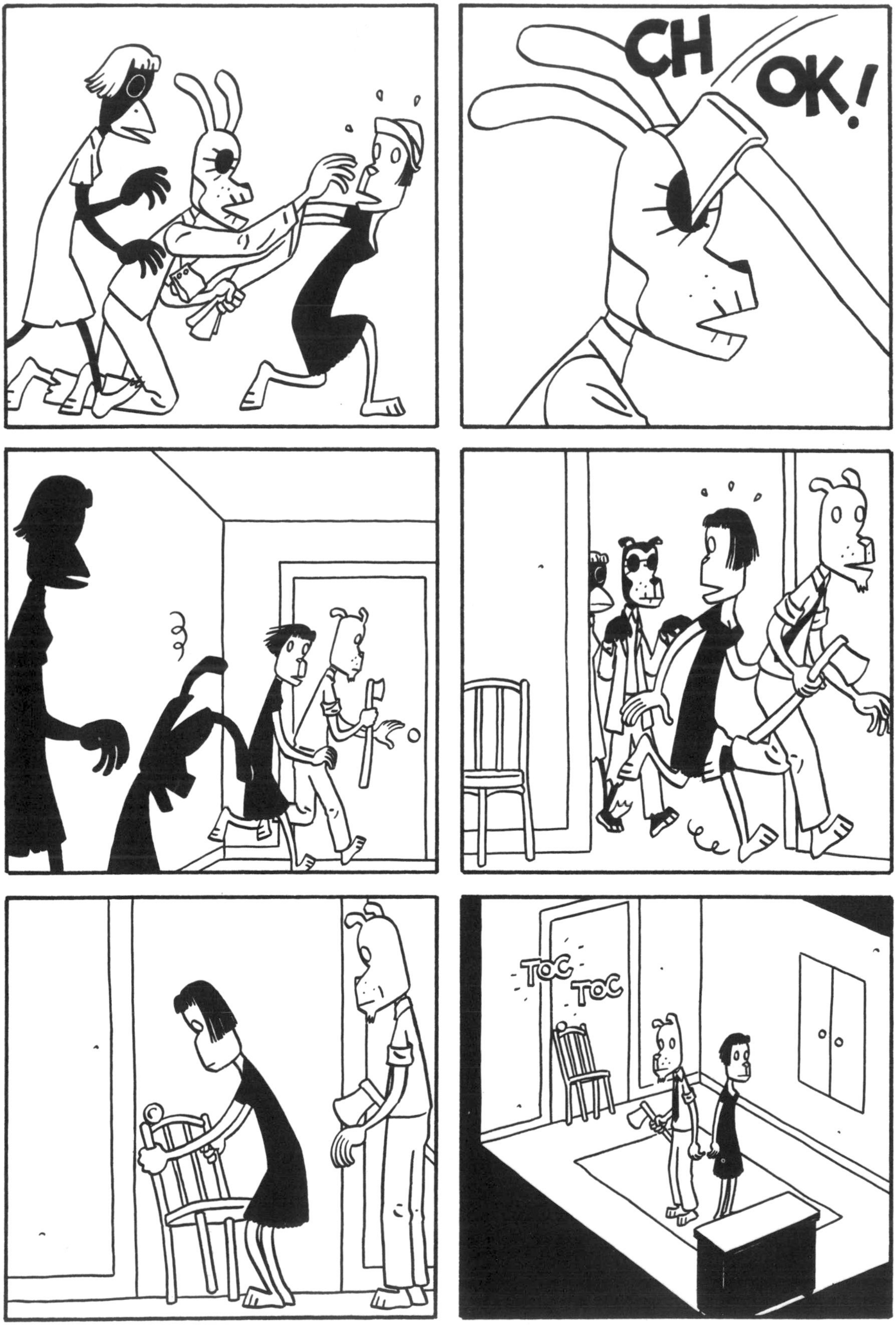
CH OK!
TOC TOC

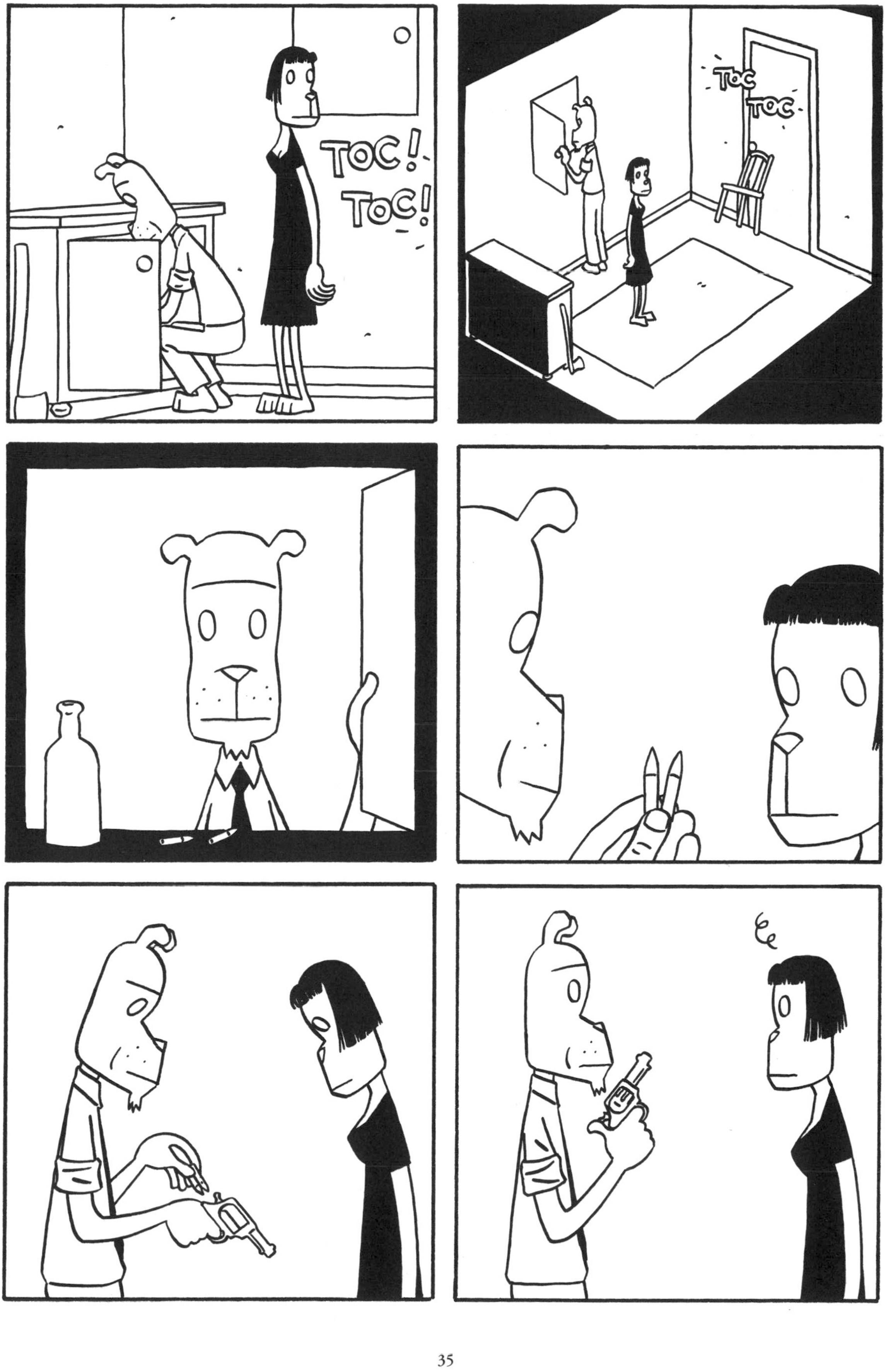
TOC!
TOC!
TOC
TOC

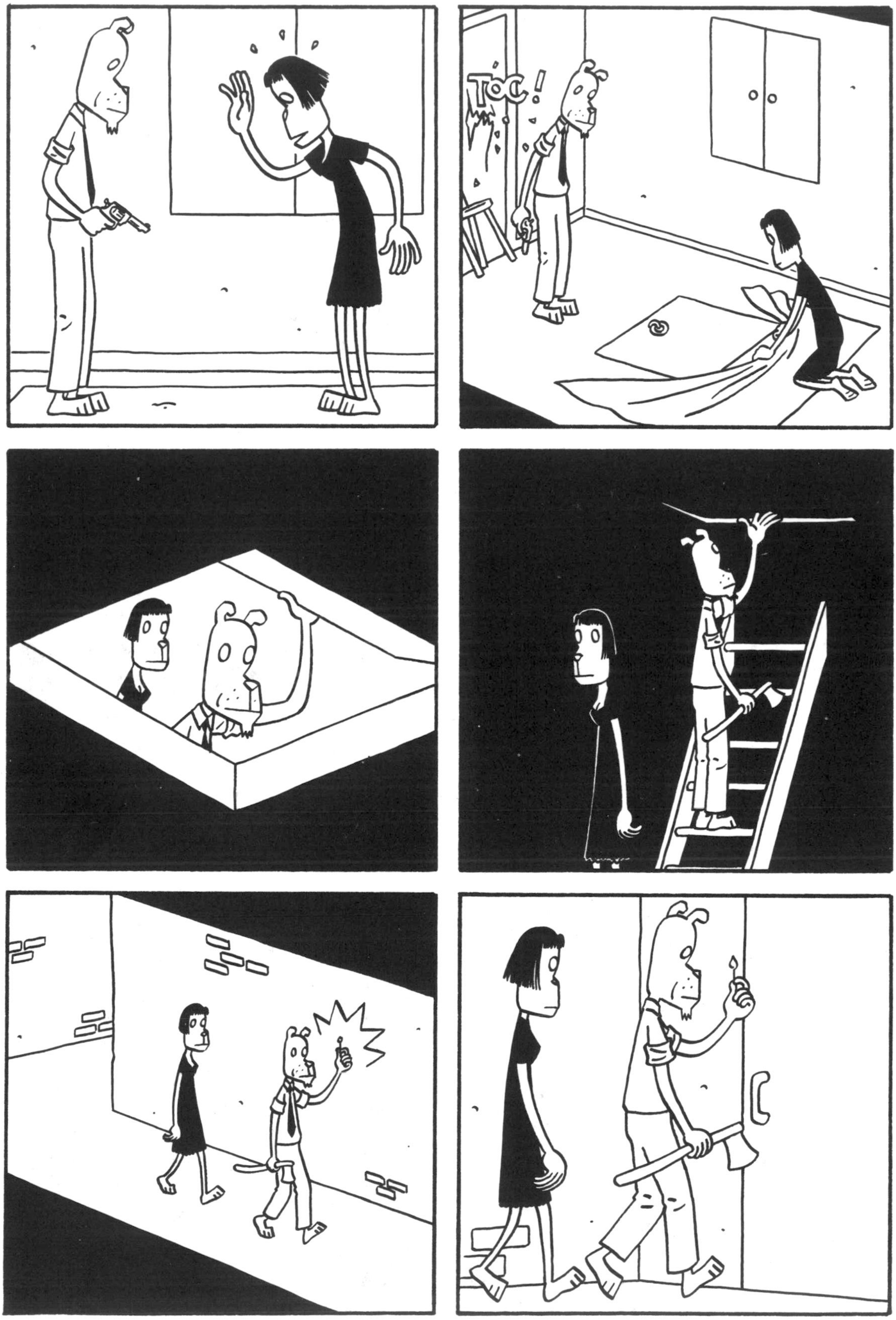
TOC!

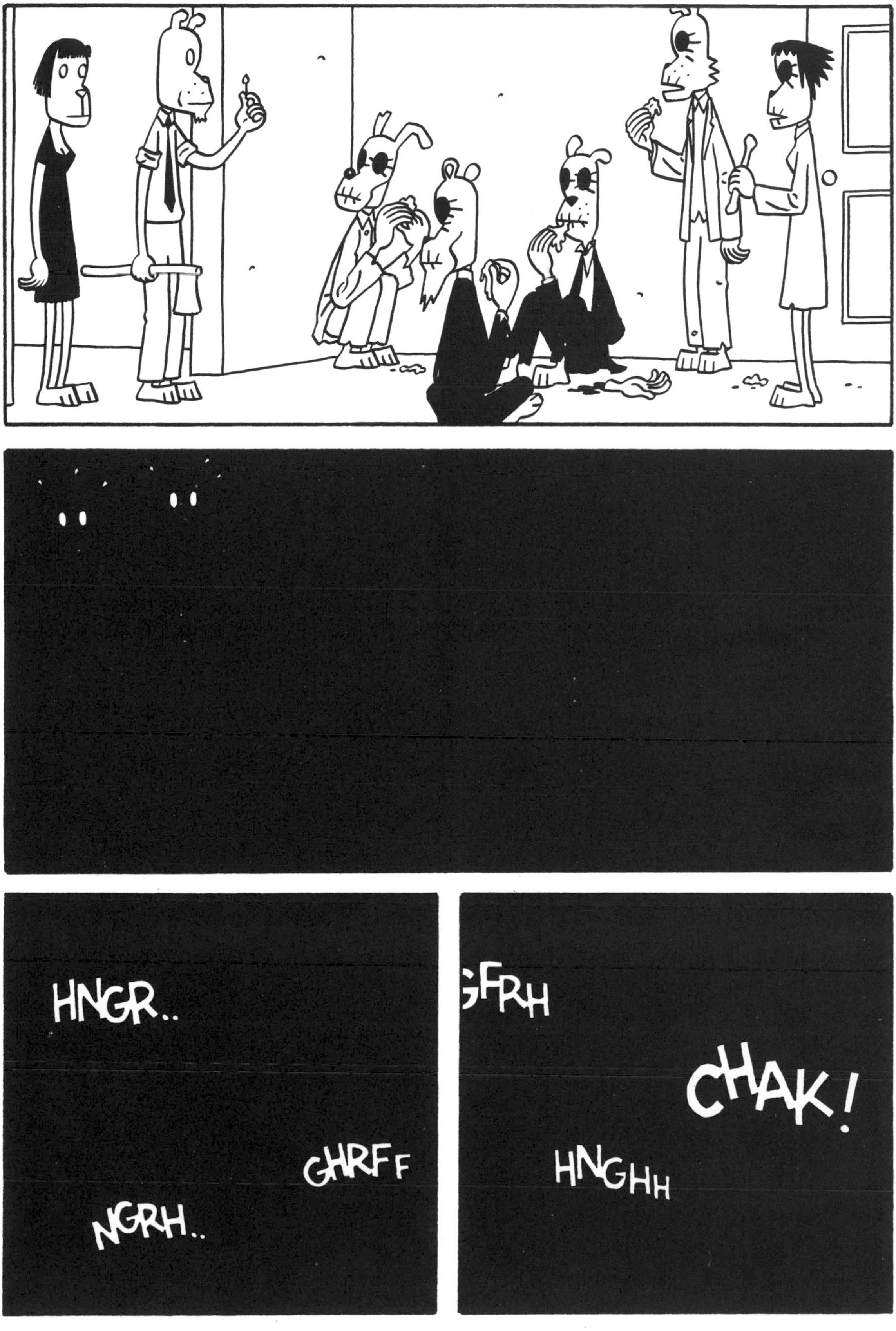
HNGR..
GHRFF
NGRH..
GFRH
CHAK!
HNGHH

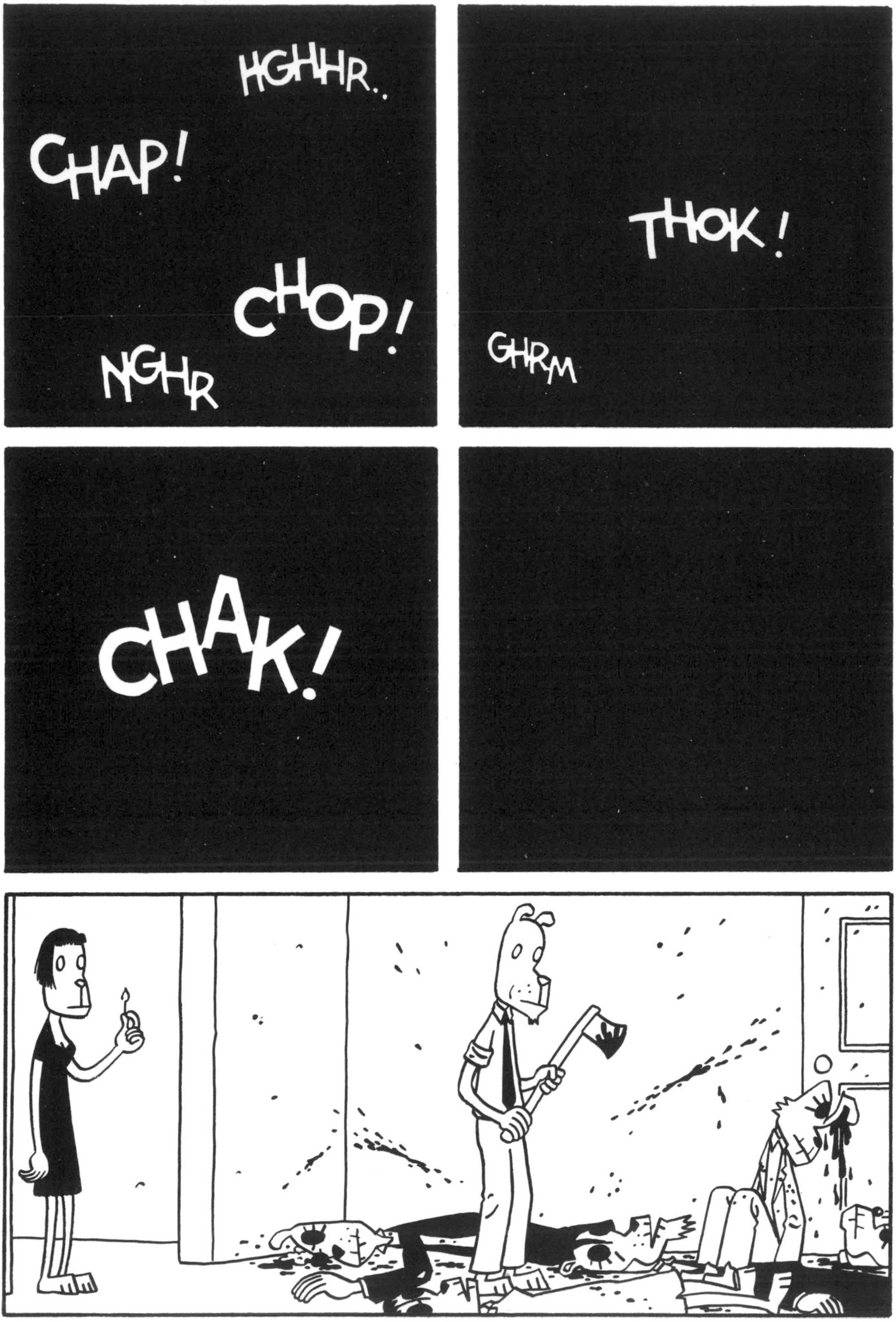
HGHHR..
CHAP!
CHOP!
NGHR
THOK!
GHRM
CHAK!

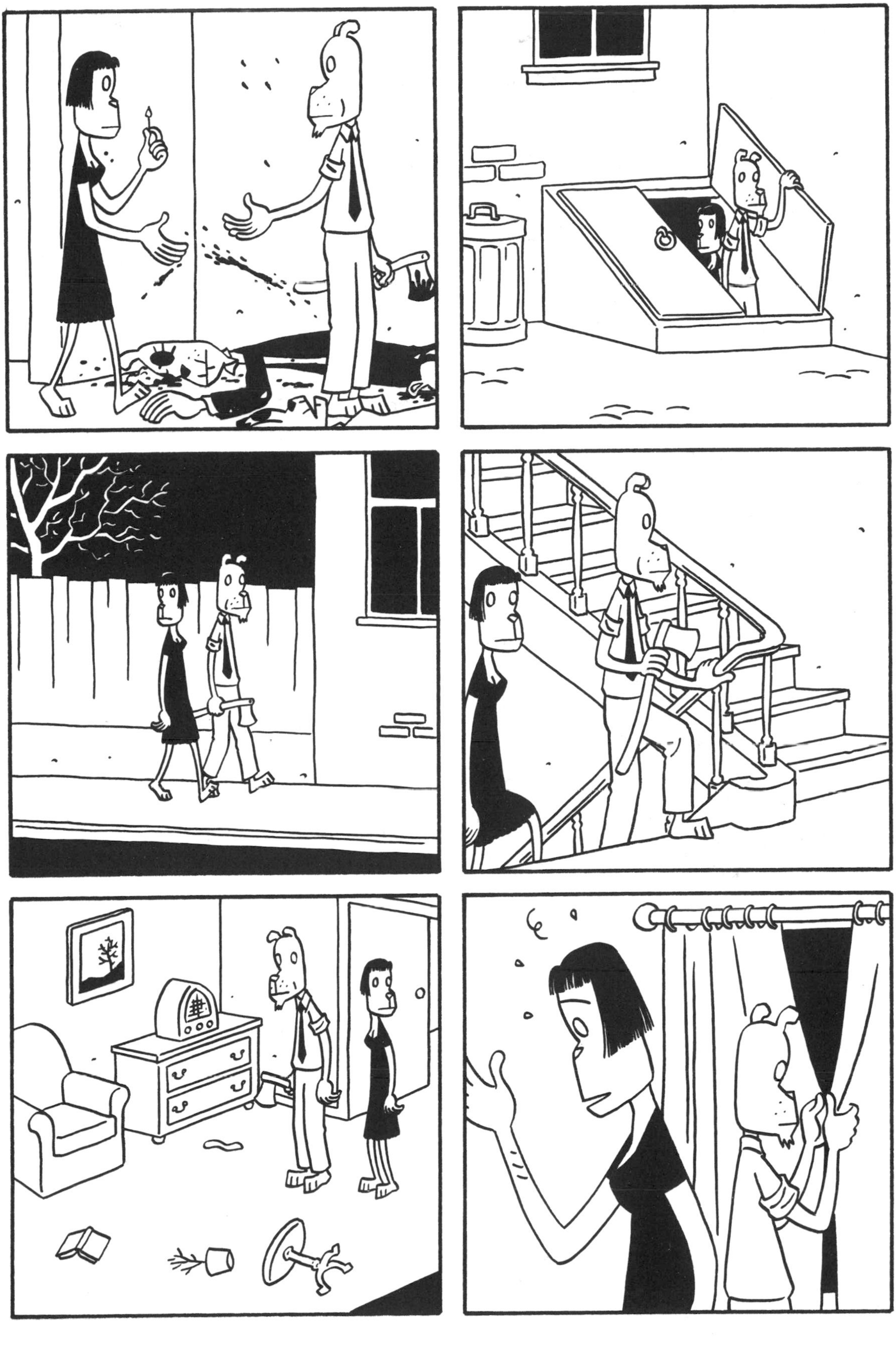

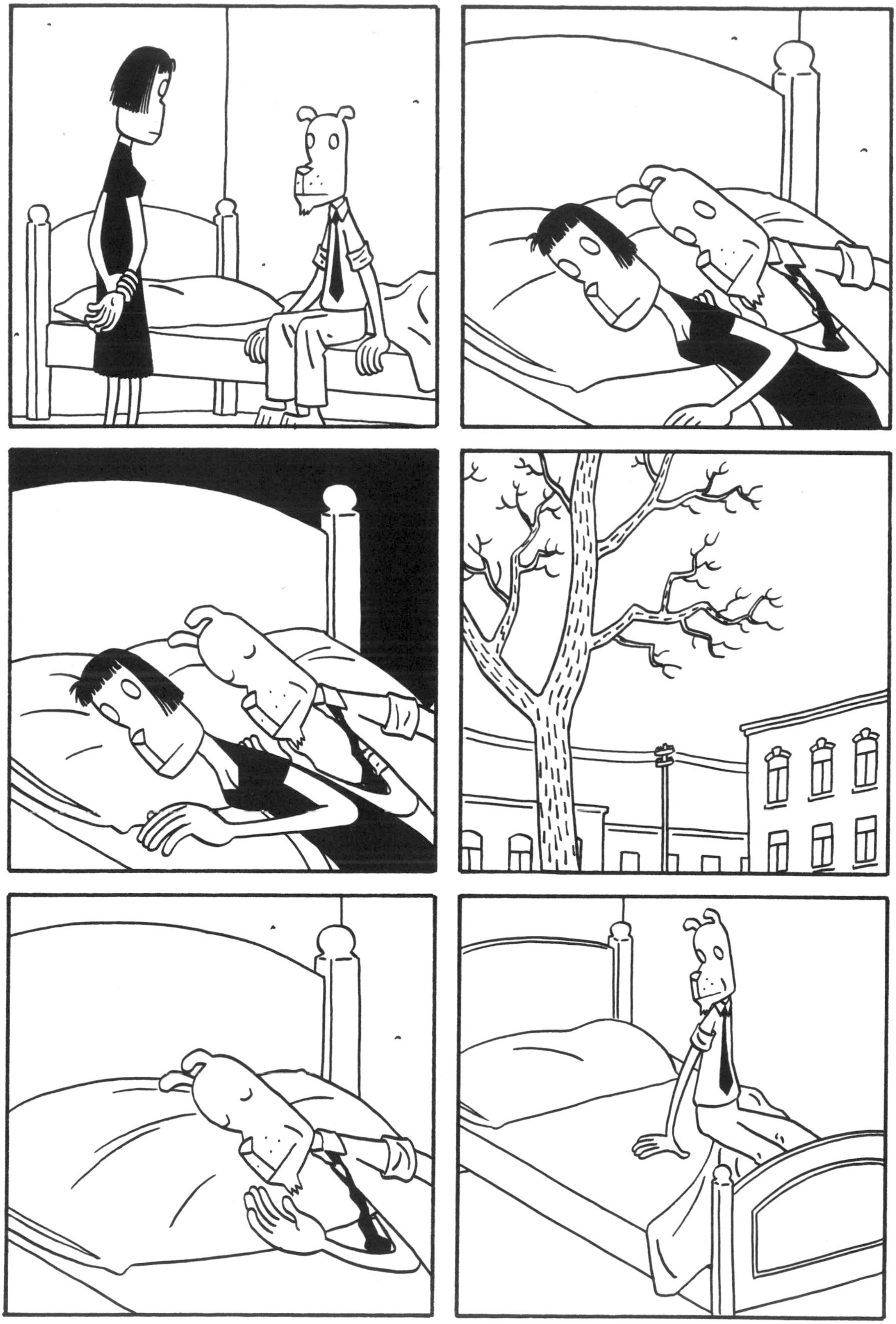

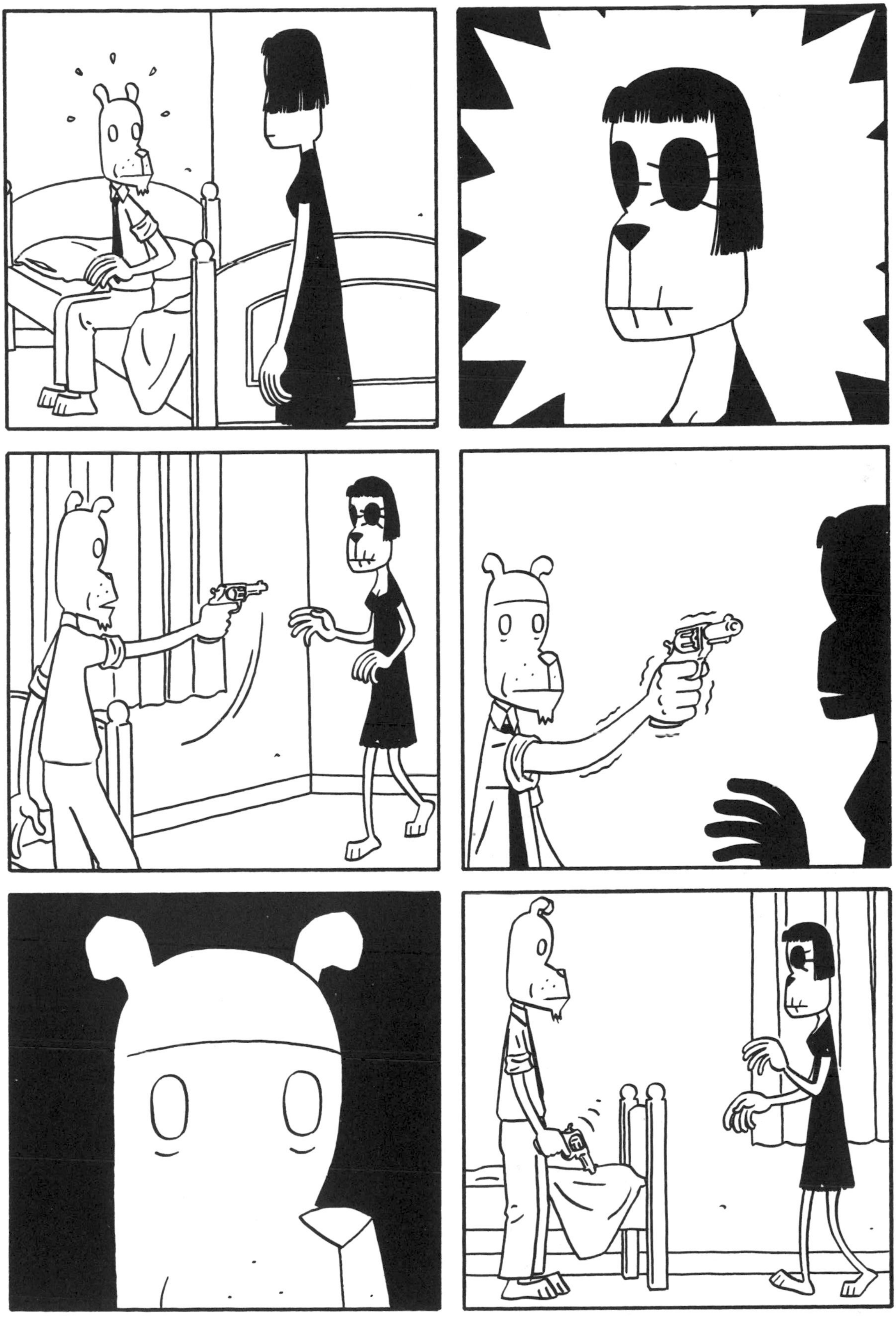

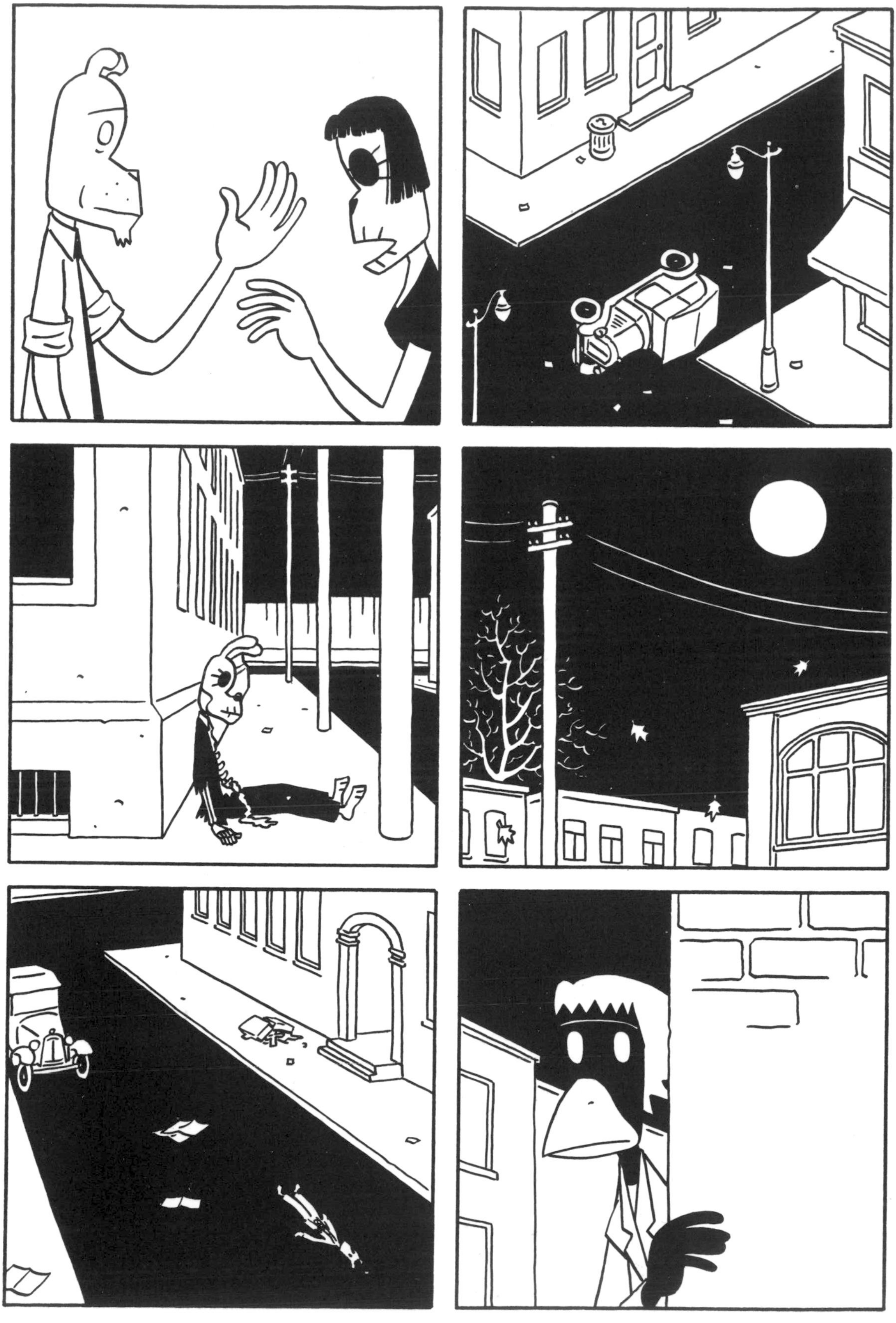

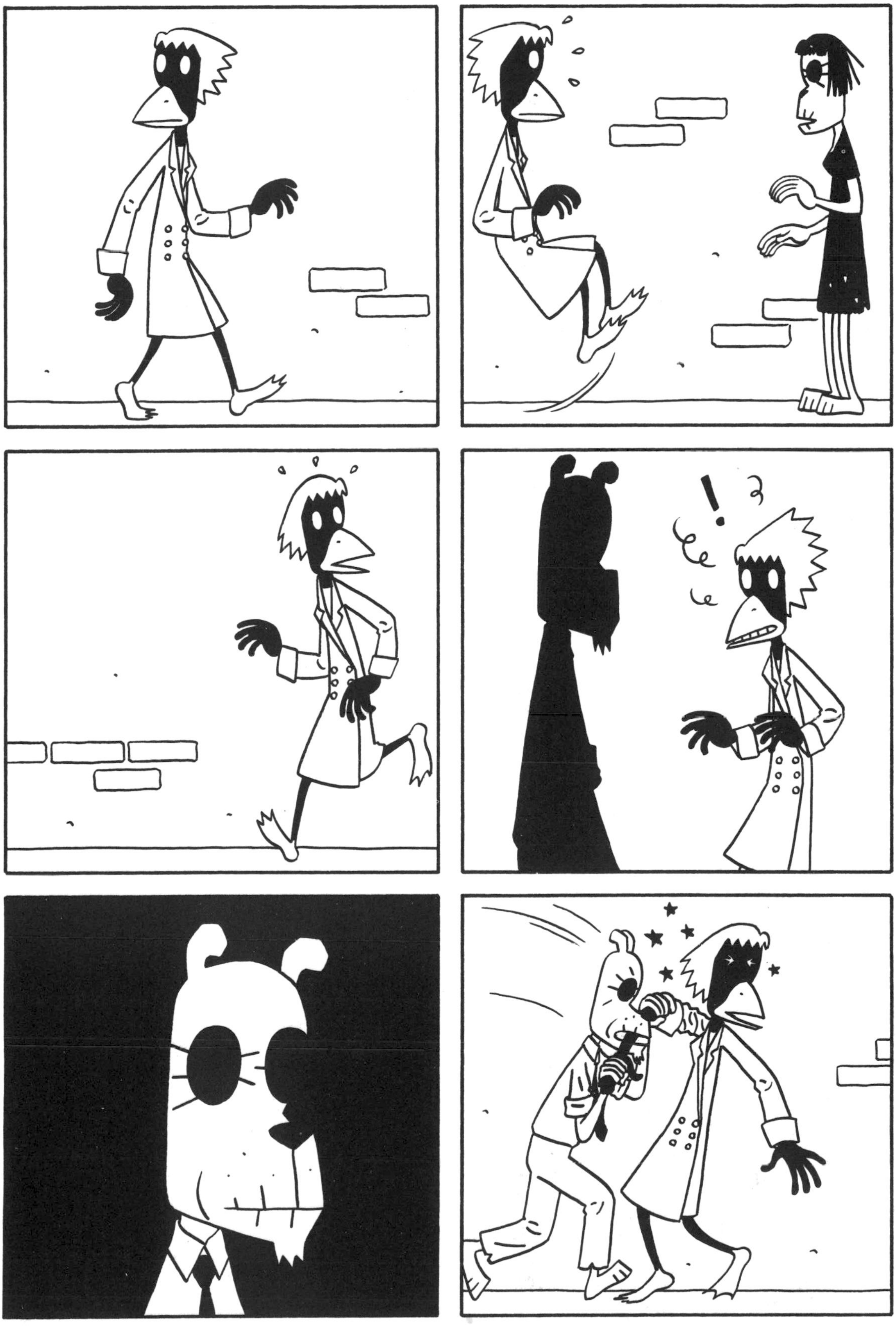

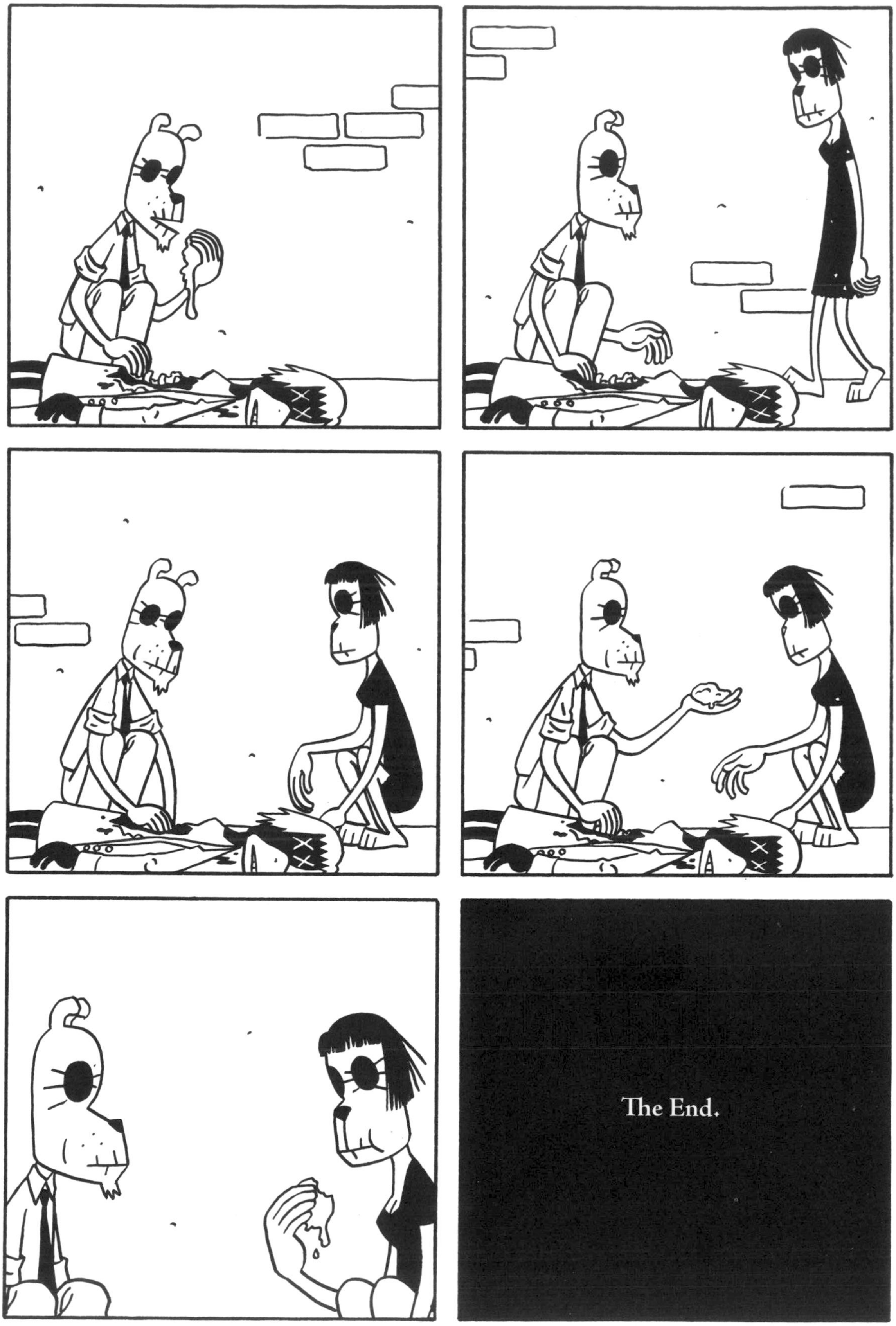
The End.